# Cypher O
### in Cairo, Kenya, C

# Elizabeth Watkins

**Pen Press Publishers**

First published in Great Britain by
Pen Press Publishers Ltd
25 Eastern Place
Brighton
BN2 1GJ


ISBN13: 978-1-906206-27-7

Printed and bound in the UK by
Cpod. Trowbridge, Wiltshire

A catalogue record of this book is available from
the British Library

Cover design by Jacqueline Abromeit

# Other books by the same author

## Jomo's Jailor: Grand Warrior of Kenya
(Britwell Books IBSN 0-9528952-0-X pbk. pp.266)

*"Skilfully and most readably put together and set in context by a younger Kenya veteran, with a Foreword from the queen of imperial history, Elspeth Huxley"* (The Spectator)

*"As fascinating a biography as could be imagined"*
(Africa Magazine, Eire)

*"A first rate and lovingly told biography"*
(Journal of the Anglo-Somali Society)

*"This is a first class biography of a man who deserved one"*
(The Overseas Pensioner)

*"This is a book to be enjoyed"*
(The International Journal of African Historical Studies)

## Oscar from Africa
(Radcliffe Press IBSN 1-85043-948-6.hbk.pp265)

*"This fascinating book ... the story of a very remarkable man, well researched and engagingly told"* (Oxford Magazine)

*"Both instructive and fascinating. It is well researched and well written"*
(Women in Kenya)

*"Essential reading for everyone interested in the colonial period in Kenya and in the operation of the colonial service"*
(The African Studies Association of Australasia and the Pacific Review)

*"Fluently and not uncritically told"* (African Affairs)

## Olga in Kenya: Repressing the Irrepressible

(Pen Press Publishers Ltd ISBN 1-905203-74-8 pp278 pbk.)

*"The enchanting story of this woman of boundless energy .... the author drags the reader across three continents, through two World Wars in the breathless chase of her mother's life"*

(Joseph Ngunjiri, The Sunday Nation, Nairobi)

*"Elizabeth Watkins has written another engrossing biography .... the book will be invaluable to the reader and historian interested in Kenya's immediate past"*

(Sir John Johnson, The Overseas Pensioner)

*"When you pick it up, you can't put it down"*

(A Reader, Oxford, UK)

*"I just finished Olga this morning. I absolutely loved it. What experiences....vey few women today are as brave"*

(A Reader, Lexington,Mass., USA)

*"I am sitting by the fire reading Olga ... and alternately laughing and crying"* ( A Reader , Henley-on-Thames,UK)

# Contents

# *Chapter* 1
## The Great Flap 1942

Tight khaki skirts, as worn by WAAFs in time of war, are not conducive to pyramid climbing, but I did not complain. Not every girl sets out to climb the Great Pyramid by moonlight on the eve of her nineteenth birthday. It was particularly hot that summer of 1942 in Cairo, the Summer of the Great Flap when the Allied troops were busy burning their secret papers in roof-top incinerators. Despite the activities of armies in retreat all round me, I was still a typical teenager, entirely absorbed in my own affairs. Tomorrow I would move one step closer to my third decade – and thank God for that. I was furious that I'd had to leave my English school at the outbreak of war, aged just sixteen, and join my parents in Kenya, where no higher education for girls was possible. I felt frustrated because I had wanted to stay on and go to university.

The evening had started in the YWCA hostel, when the only other occupant, Janet, tried to wake me by shaking my iron bedstead.

"Do wake up, Nairobi," she said, "it's seven o'clock and the men have arrived." She had tried to wake me earlier and sounded exasperated at my tardiness.

"I'll be down in ten minutes," I said, streaking for the shower. How easy dressing had become, I thought as I returned dripping. I possessed just one suitcase of clothes, three khaki uniforms, and the only choice in the whole outfit was panties or knickers. I sighed. My old school knickers with elastic round the legs – 'glamour killers', as they were called– were much hotter than panties but glamour killers it would have to be if I was going to climb a pyramid in a uniform skirt.

I paused to fit the narrow rank badges of an assistant section officer over the straps of a new poplin shirt, and took a clean khaki drill skirt from my suitcase. At least the skirt had two pleats back and front and was not straight like the blue ones. I quite liked wearing uniform, for in all my life there had only been two years when I had not worn one and that had not been long enough to learn to enjoy choosing my own clothes. Still less did I like those passed down by my elder sisters.

"Boyfriends too silly, dresses too frilly," I would mutter under my breath as another hand-me-down came my way. At least tonight my clothes would not be too frilly, and I remembered Ken as a pleasant young man on the few occasions I had met him. I pulled on thick lisle stockings and laced up ugly black walking shoes left over from my schooldays. What were my family doing now, at this moment, at home in Kenya? Would they remember it was my birthday and drink my health?

Almost overwhelmed by a longing for them all, I asked myself why I had left home to join up at all. It was nice to think I'd been motivated by patriotism but I was honest enough to recognize my longing for independence, for freedom from the constrictions of family life. Yet even in the ten weeks I had been away I had learned that the constraints of service life were more limiting than those of my comparatively liberal home. Where I worked or lived, what I wore or ate, whom I met or went out with, were all determined by the huge war machine in which I had become the smallest of small cogs.

A hasty look in the mirror told me my face had the scrubbed, shiny schoolgirl look rather than that of the sophisticated woman of the world I aspired to be. But there was no point in using makeup, it would be sweated off in ten minutes. I ran a wet comb through blonde flyaway hair, buttoned an identity card and money into my left breast pocket, and strapped on my watch. It was just eight minutes since I had been called. As I slung my tin helmet over my left shoulder and picked up my cap, it was time to wonder what the night would bring and ponder on the strangeness of a birthday party consisting of complete strangers.

In that wartime city there were thousands of lonely young men eager to take a girl out. Ken, an officer in a well-known Scots regiment, was an ex-boyfriend of my eldest sister. He had contacted me while on leave, and promised this visit to the Great Pyramid for my birthday. He would bring two other officers, I two other girls. I had invited two girls from the hostel where I lived, but that very morning they had been evacuated from the city. Later in the day Janet, a New Zealand nurse, had become separated from her unit and had moved in. Ken was the only person I had met before. I had somehow expected to see him resplendent in the tartan trews he had worn to escort my sister to balls in Nairobi. Instead, all three young men wore washed-out khaki, and scuffed desert boots. They had the tired, dispirited look losing armies always have. The war was not going well on the Western Front; the fall of Malta was expected at any moment.

As we set out for dinner the sun was setting, the air was slightly cooler, and the full moon was already visible. It was just the night for climbing the Great Pyramid. Just the night for Jerry too. Already there was desultory ack-ack fire from the outskirts of the town. We ate dinner at a roof top restaurant, gobbling down the food, hurrying the waiters. We knew that if we dallied, the sirens would sound and we would be jostled into a shelter, the evening spoilt. Cairo was never bombed, only the military units around it, but there was always fear that it might be. On each chair round the table hung the regulation tin helmet, and in each helmet rested a uniform cap. Just before we left, one of the men pinched my helmet and poured into it the remaining drink on the table, and the hat was passed round from mouth to mouth. Other tables joined in, drink was added and my helmet circulated. The whole floor sang Happy Birthday, closely followed by:

*"Why was she born so beautiful,*
*"Why was she born at all?"*

I was still too gauche to respond with anything but embarrassment, fortunately hidden when the helmet, still half full of drink, was forced down on to my head. Soon five of us were crowded into the little open sports car speeding across the desert, the wind blowing the smell of alcohol from my hair. At least it was only alcohol, and the helmet was metal. They did far worse to the WAAF caps of new officers in an RAF Mess.

Mina House Hotel crouched low among its oasis of trees. The moon was at just the angle to throw a giant shadow of the pyramid on the sand, making it loom over us larger than ever. The steps between each tier of stone were huge, waist-high; here and there a stone had crumbled, or niches had been cut, so that a reasonably fit person could haul themselves up.

We were the only visitors there that night. The rabble of dragomans at the bottom of the pyramid had insisted we hire four guides – customarily women needed two men to haul them up, one pulling, one pushing. Janet, who was permitted to wear slacks, leapt up like a gazelle, following one of the guides, and the men started racing to keep up with them. The remaining guides concentrated on me, hampered as I was by my unforgiving skirt. I too was determined to be independent, and even more determined not to reveal the shameful glamour killers. My father had taught me to vault gates, legs sideways and together as I jumped, and now I found this ability most useful, clambering up a few niches, vaulting sideways, rising to my feet, and repeating the procedure. There was a danger of losing balance and rolling down backwards, but I reckoned the two dragomans standing below me, ready to push, would catch me. The sweat poured from us, the soft sand-stone yielded under our probing hands and feet, dust from the others fell on me, and then the three young men were bending over, reaching down to haul me up the last stone to the top.

The moon shed a kind of bluish light, which softened the harshness of the desert scenery. The sand stretched to the horizon, broken only by the low hills of Cairo and Helwan. Cairo, only half blacked out, was a gentle blur. Andy, the wittiest of the three young men, the one who had kept us laughing throughout dinner, pointed North where pinpoints of moving light showed the road leading from Mina House up to Alexandria and the front. There was sadness not laughter in his voice as he said:

"That's where we will be this time tomorrow. I hope it's as quiet as this!" I knew from my work (no one had of course mentioned it) that their unit was the next one to go in against Rommel. Not having seen the British blitz, I did not think it was quiet at all. German reconnaissance planes were cradled in the weaving fingers of spotlights. Ack-ack deafened us as it broke in bright stars below the planes. Ken produced a bottle of champagne he had lugged up in his pocket, and, sitting in a row with our legs dangling over the edge, everyone drank my health yet again, direct from the tepid bottle. We hid the empty on the top and, sweating even more profusely as a result of the alcohol, we clambered quickly down again. I had to be back to go on night watch at half past one in the cypher office of Combined Headquarters.

**4**

When we had driven out, the only traffic had been convoys driving from Cairo to the front. Now, after midnight, we mingled with two streams of traffic. Hundreds of civilian vehicles were streaming into Cairo down the road from Alexandria, bedding and possessions tied on top. At the same time local Cairenes were packing up in their hundreds and moving to Ismailia, further East, further from the Germans. Rommel and his armies were less than forty miles of smooth flat sand from Alexandria; Alexandria, less than eighty miles of excellent communications – road, river and rail – from Cairo. The great flap was felt by the locals as much as by the occupying armies.

As we drove back, hot and crowded in the small open car, I thought how romantic, how exciting life had become, and wondered where the next party would take me. I did not know this was to be my last party for a long time – the next day a curfew was introduced. It was also the last time I thought of war as romantic. Two weeks later, two of those three young men were dead.

# Chapter 2
## Night Watch at the Metropole

The RAF cypher office was then in the old Hotel Metropole, and very busy it was when I came on duty after climbing the Great Pyramid. In one large room half a dozen typex machines (more complex copies of the famous Enigma) clattered incessantly; in another smaller one, half a dozen girls sat round tables with the cypher books in front of them, patiently turning words into figures, and then subtracting those figures from columns of numbers. I was among them. It was close, tiring, finicky work.

At this stage of the war book-cyphers were rapidly disappearing but were still used by all the mobile units, and the units retreating from Rommel were very mobile indeed. During the day messages to be encoded came in faster than we could send them out; at night we were decyphering messages that streamed in from other theatres of war, other time zones.

I came on duty with a sort of dread expectation in the pit of my stomach. What would the news be this time? It seemed to be always at night that big news came in: what was happening at the front now so near, or back home in Blighty, or in Russia, or in the Far East. We all knew the eyes of the world were on us – Greece had been evacuated, Cyprus and Crete had fallen. Was Cairo going to fall to Rommel's army?

One of the tasks faced by cyphers is to ensure that the groups of numbers so laboriously created from words can somehow be turned back into words by those for whom they are intended. Fresh from cypher school, I was put on the 'corruption' table in the book room to sort out those whose numbers would not yield sense.

"Can't think what has happened with this squadron – every signal they have sent seems to be corrupt!" I belly-ached.

The officer in charge of the book room was suddenly standing by me. She was a thin girl with dark circles under her eyes, her hair scraggy in the heat, her face sweaty and innocent of makeup. She was quite old, she must have been at least twenty-seven. She used my nickname, not my surname, to soften the reproof.

"Nairobi, you mustn't even think like that! Try to think what it's like out there in the desert, Jerry bombing you all the time, and there you are retreating all day, trying to get a message out at night, no proper lights, working in a truck, being bombed, packing up to move, losing your friends."

It was only later that I heard her boyfriend was a pilot with the squadron from whom the corrupt message came. He never came back. She decyphered the casualty list herself and never said a word, nor missed an hour's work.

RAF cyphers did all the messages for Combined Headquarters as well as RAF ones, and one never knew what would be spelt out next. Usually it was something mundane: lists of spare parts for the maintenance unit, casualty and compassionate leave lists, the regular daily "mayflys" which gave a unit's strength and the weekly reports each had to submit. Sometimes it was more exciting: reports on battles, recommendations for awards for bravery, a summary of events on other fronts. Occasionally there was a message of outstanding importance: an analysis of battle by a commander-in-chief and Winston Churchill's reply; a discussion of future strategy. All that night every message spoke of defeat and retreat. It was difficult to keep cheerful.

My father had sent me £20 for my birthday: a great sacrifice for him, two months' pay for me, a small fortune indeed. He had written in a touching letter that when he was young he had never had enough money and now he wanted me to be able to enjoy myself, to go on leave. Leave? In Cairo in 1942? Instead of taking the transport truck home from night duty, I walked to the Bank of Egypt to see if the money had arrived.

To my surprise, a noisy crowd was waiting outside. The doors opened at 8 a.m. and I was carried in on a tide of excited Egyptian businessmen, each trying to withdraw his money before the Germans arrived. It was my first experience of panic. I was jam-packed somewhere in the middle of the huge marble hall, usually so empty and cool, now so hot and airless that I felt ill and wondered how I could get out again. Fresh air seemed more important than money.

"Good God, it's June, isn't it?" a voice near me said. "You've cut your pigtails off!" The voice belonged to a plump young man, one Richard Dimbleby, nephew of an old family friend, whom I had not seen for six years. He was now in khaki, a captain's pips on his shoulders.

"How clever of you to recognize me! It must be at least six years!"

"You look just the same!" he retorted. At eighteen this was not a compliment. I did not want to look like a plump twelve-year-old in a gym tunic, but before I could remonstrate he said, "Do you want the withdrawals counter? You'll never get through by yourself. I'll give you a push." He put his considerable bulk behind me and, using me as a battering ram and his powerful arms as oars, he propelled us both through the protesting mass.

In five minutes we reached the counter where an unshaven middle-aged man with a droopy moustache and sweat trickling down his face was shouting through the guichet in French to the clerk to hurry up, each shout enveloping us in a strong wave of garlic. The clerk went on counting out paper money, tatty Egyptian notes. He recounted them methodically before pushing the heap across the counter. The man snatched at the notes with such force that several fell to pieces in his hands. He burst into noisy tears, brandishing the pieces in both hands and screaming abuse at the clerk through his sobs. Unperturbed, the clerk turned to me, and took only a few minutes to fetch my £20. My notes, I saw with satisfaction, were in reasonable condition. Richard remained standing behind me, his bulk sheltering me from the pushing crowds; he dealt with the clerk over my head. When we both had our money buttoned into inside pockets, he turned round, told me to hold tight to his shoulders and this time used a swimming motion to tow me out. We stood on the steps for a few moments; even the hot sticky air of a June morning in Cairo seemed refreshing.

The streets were crowded, a polyglot cross-section of masculinity. Egyptian beggars in dirty striped nightshirts, dirt-encrusted small boys in the same nightshirts, dodging in and out of the traffic as they chased the little horse-drawn *garis* favoured by young officers. There were troops and uniforms from all over the world, *askaris* from Kenya, hulking great soldiers from Australia, Canada, New Zealand, small brown men from India, black and brown and white, officers and men, all reduced to the same common denominator by much-washed khaki shorts, ill-fitting khaki tunics, long stockings, brown suede desert boots of the kind known as brothel creepers. Egyptian businessmen, sleek, oily, solemn, strode about in their smart linen suits among the shabby young soldiers. Only women were lacking. It was still too early for the prostitutes, and ordinary Cairene women did not then frequent the streets except when wrapped in black from head to foot, like members of some enclosed religious order.

Outside the bank another acquaintance, Charles Davis, came up to us. He was a South African accountant my parents had befriended in Kenya in the Ethiopian campaign. It seemed a lifetime away. He recognized me immediately and came striding up.

"What are you doing here?" he shouted in a strong South African accent. "All our girls have gone! You should go too!"

"We'll go if headquarters go," I replied, knowing that I must not mention even to fellow officers that Advanced HQ had already left the desert for the Canal zone, so were now behind us, Rear HQ; and that we in turn were on stand-by to leapfrog over them into Palestine. "And I'd rather stay," I added. Stories of some five hundred South African women evacuated south to Luxor, crowded into one hotel without their kit and with nothing to do, were filtering back to us. Luxor in June and July is one of the hottest places in the world; on the second day the hotel had run out of water.

"There's a brave girl," said Charles patronizingly, "and we're all here to defend you!" He patted his gun dramatically – all troops were armed at that moment.

"I don't think you need worry," I said cockily, "I can look after myself." And I patted the bulge under my own tunic. It was not policy for women to carry firearms, but that very week we had been taken to the roof of the Metropole and shown how to use them. Anyone who had a gun was permitted to carry it. Recently news had come through that women officers in both the ATS and the WAAF had at last been given full commissions. It was the first time women had been commissioned and thus our legal status had changed; if we were captured we would be treated as prisoners of war rather than camp followers;. It also meant that we could be court-martialled for serious offences, such as breaking the rulings on secrecy. It was hinted that it might be better for cypher officers not to be taken prisoners, and we were shown how to handle firearms and even shoot ourselves should it become necessary. I had felt very superior, knowing it all in advance, for my father had taught me before I left home. I had never thought it strange that a father should teach a much-loved daughter how to fight off a rape attack, how to use a firearm, and how to take her own life.

Richard took me to Groppis, the well-known coffee shop, for an iced coffee. We decided to have it in the garden, but were told it was not open. Later, from the window of the ladies' loo, I discovered why: in the garden they were busy painting signs in German to welcome the German army. Groppis were not the only owners to prepare for the invasion; my hairdresser also had a German sign ready to hang up. After all, the Germans were only a hundred and twenty miles from Cairo. As I walked back to the hostel I was imagining what the street might look like in a week's time

The various allied headquarters in Cairo were also preparing. For days every office had been burning every possible bit of paper rather than risk it falling into German hands. Smoke rose in columns from flat roofs and fragments of paper ash hung in the still air above central Cairo like black snowflakes. At cypher school we had burnt as we learnt, never keeping a scrap of paper, and now I had been put in charge of an incinerator we were to take with us if we were evacuated, so we could burn as we ran.

By the time I arrived at the hostel it was after 10 a.m.; I had been on the go all night and had only managed a brief nap the day before. Now all leave had been suspended the hostel would be quiet today. It was intended for people on leave, not residents, and I was only allowed to live there because until two weeks ago my aunt had been the warden. When I had first arrived in Cairo early in April, my uncle, an Admiral, had insisted that I stay with him rather than go to a hotel with the girls who had joined up with me. He was the Senior Naval Officer at Combined Operations HQ; and had a luxurious flat on Gezirah Island, complete with a Maltese servant to look after him.

My aunt had wanted to join him for a few months while he was ashore in Cairo, and had obtained a passage from Britain by undertaking to run the main YWCA hostel. For my first two months in Cairo I lived a double life, in a luxurious flat attending every kind of entertainment at senior officer level in my free time – lunch with the Kinnears at the British Embassy, dinner with Lord Moyne – whilst attending cypher school as the lowest form of animal life during the day. This contrast had at times been embarrassing. At one particular command performance at the opera house, we were invited by Lord Kinnear's party to the main box in the theatre, buying programmes from the most senior WAAF officers as we went in. It was a charity show, and tickets were not even available for junior officers and other ranks. I was not doing anything illegal, but hated to make myself so conspicuous.

Barely had I completed cypher school than my uncle was recalled to Britain to set up the Combined Organization operation that would, two years later, lead to the invasion of Normandy. As a very senior officer, he travelled by air, so the journey from Cairo to Southampton via Khartoum, West Africa, Gibraltar and Lisbon took only a week. My aunt and I moved to the YWCA hostel. She had to wait her turn to travel by sea; for the second time in less than a year she set out on the dangerous eight-week voyage right round Africa. She thought she was lucky, other wives could not travel to be with their husbands.

I too was lucky to be allowed to live in the hostel although the place was far from ideal. I had to share a room with ever-changing girls from a wide range of services, which fact greatly limited my opportunities for daytime sleep after night duty. Now all leave in the Middle East had been suspended, nearly all service women evacuated, and the hostel had become ghostly quiet. Nor could we escape this morgue, for the newly introduced curfew meant we could not go out. Once the servants and staff had gone, Janet and I were alone in the huge old building.

Until now it had been just a hostel, a place run for our benefit in an unfortunate war. That night we looked around us and realized the beauty of the place, the well-proportioned rooms, the elegant Moorish windows, the carved doors and shutters, the curving central staircase. The drabness came from the army issue furniture at its starkest, iron bedsteads, wooden chests. Now we tried to see it as it might once have been.

"This would make a splendid palm room, with potted plants and little tables!" said Janet as we fetched ourselves water from the cooler in the cafeteria.

"There should be a large gilt mirror here, so guests could see themselves as they arrived for a reception," I said from the top of the first-floor staircase.

"Look at that marvellous ceiling!" Janet was in the ping-pong room. "The grand piano should stand here, and there would be family portraits on it."

"And a ring of chairs round a rosewood table. Louis Fifteenth? Chippendale?" I was showing off. Janet was a nurse from New Zealand and I a school girl from Kenya. Neither of us knew what we were talking about as we walked round the building, furnishing it to our taste.

"Where shall we put the nursery?" I enquired.

"It was here, where the windows are barred." We were on the second floor and she led me into a large room which now held six beds. It was where she was sleeping. "Why don't you move in with me, for company. It's eerie here alone."

"I usually sleep here," I told her as she followed me up to the roof garden, "when I have the whole night in bed. It's so much cooler. See, I hide my camp bed here by day, and then unroll it and hitch my mosquito net to that hook."

"It's dangerous, with Jerry overhead!" Janet commented. Planes were droning over now, with the fingers of spotlights chasing them.

"I did wake up the other morning with a bit of flak on my bed, tore this hole in my net," I admitted, "but it's wonderfully cool. And quiet. No one storming in, in the wee hours."

"That won't do. Move to my room. We can both sleep in tomorrow."

The following evening A-watch was again on duty. Before every watch, transport came round to fetch us from our various quarters around Cairo. The ubiquitous three-ton truck had benches down either side, but there was rarely room for everyone to sit, so we stood up clinging to the bars, swaying and jogging through the traffic, with similar trucks of soldiers whistling and waving as we went by. Now that Germans were flying over the city, all transport had to be covered with canvas, so the heat inside became almost insupportable. Fresh from a cold shower as one might be, sweat was pouring and clothes sodden by the time we arrived on duty fifteen minutes later. There was no end to it; one lived in perpetually damp clothes, and I was not the only one to suffer from prickly heat, a maddening itch all over the body.

We had been given a code word which would warn us that Rear Headquarters was about to be evacuated. A few days later I found that word in my mailbox. I hurried through the instructions I had been given, packing and stowing my camp kit in the baggage room, discarding civvies, taking only khaki and one blue uniform in my canvas air case, putting my blue greatcoat ready to carry as instructed. As I looked ruefully at my small possessions, I asked myself what I should do if holed up in some hotel like the South African women still were. I must take my books – I only had about a dozen, some I had just bought in Cairo, some my father had sent me, including my favourite anthology of poetry. Then there was my photograph album, a notebook. I opened my case, took out the blue uniform, crammed it down the sleeves of the great coat, filled up the space in the case with books, and tried to look nonchalant as I clambered into the bus (a proper bus this time and not a three-ton truck) clutching my greatcoat and heavy suitcase.

I need not have worried. Everyone was laden with the things she could not bear to abandon. One girl in midsummer Cairo was carrying a fur coat as well as her Air Force blue one; another a songbird in a cage; a third a huge china ornament. There were portable typewriters, gramophones, packages of all shapes and sizes. By comparison my well-stuffed greatcoat was nothing.

We were to work through our watch and then assemble in the canteen for a meal, after which the bus, with the afternoon watch already on board, would be waiting to evacuate us through the cool of the night. We would pack up half the machines and take them with us; the last watch to leave would bring the remainder. I wondered that defeat and retreat should be so well planned.

There were more messages than ever that evening and we worked on in silence, heads down, shirts sticking to our backs, paper sticking to our wrists, avoiding each other's eyes, knowing fear was contagious. Was Egypt going to fall? So many places had fallen during the previous twelve months. We did not know our destination, only that we were not going south. As we could not go north or west, it must be east. For how long would Palestine be safe? What if the Germans broke through at Stalingrad and came down? Where would we all end? What was it like in the bag? Was it really better for a woman cypher officer to shoot herself? What was courage? Was Hitler going to win? Already I could decypher book cyphers mechanically, leaving the rest of my brain to chase fruitless thoughts round and round.

Suddenly there was a stir. The chief WAAF, a short dumpy woman in her early forties, came into the room. I had spoken to her only once, when she'd congratulated each of us on passing cypher school and thus gaining our commissions, and given us a pep talk. Now all pretence at humour, all bonhomie was drained from her face, lined and red-eyed with strain.

"All right, girls, you'll not be going after all. You can go home tonight as usual. Your transport is waiting for you."

"Why so early?" I asked, and she glared at me. She thought I was being sarcastic, for when I looked at my watch it was past two o'clock, we were an hour overdue. How could the night have gone so quickly?

"You will be going to the new TME centre very shortly," she said and was gone. We knew the letters stood for Telecommunications Centre Middle East. None of us knew where it was. We did not have telecommunication centres in those days. It took a while to work out what the word meant.

# Chapter 3
## Hole in the Ground

The new telecommunications centre at Heliopolis was only about twelve miles from the centre of Cairo, situated underground in the first piece of open desert after the suburb of Heliopolis. The underground rooms, nicknamed The Hole, had been ready for some months, but on three separate occasions the air-conditioning plant needed to equip it had been sunk on the way out from Britain. Air-conditioning was little known on our side of the Atlantic in those days. Now the situation was considered so grave, that air-conditioning or none, we had to move and move quickly. Working underground in the desert in midsummer without air-conditioning was an experiment. Nobody knew how hot the underground offices would be once we and our heat-making machines had moved in, nor how competent we would be when working there.

Watch by watch, we were transferred to the new camp with a quiet efficiency. It seemed to me miraculous that about eighty women, forty men, and several truckloads of top-secret equipment could be packed up, moved, and reassembled without even an hour's interruption to the work. We normally worked four shifts of six hours on and twelve hours off, so that when you came off the dawn shift at 7.30, you had a glorious thirty-six free hours ahead of you, a whole night in bed. Since the introduction of a curfew we had moved to a partial three-watch system: coming off at 7.30 in the morning, half of us had to go on duty again that evening from 7.30 until 1.30 a.m. to help with the evening rush of work. This meant that daytime sleep was essential, but as the weather

**15**

became hotter in the Cairene summer, it became more difficult to sleep during the day. Our sick list grew longer but the work never abated.

Our camp had been heavily camouflaged. Sandbanks had been thrown up all round, and nets stretched over many buildings. Our living quarters were lines of concrete barracks, indescribably bleak on the harsh sand, each block with small two-bedded rooms giving onto an open corridor. A large, squat three-room building provided three large mess rooms; in the centre stood 'ablutions', a block with bucket latrines and showers. There were two latrines at the end of each block and a water point. It was not luxury, but even the grandmothers among us did not grumble; everyone except myself had a man somewhere up at the front, mostly Airforce men. The men at TME, even the Commanding Officer, all slept under canvas.

Less than a mile from us there had been a New Zealand hospital which had been evacuated. One of the nurses had been running a women's riding club, mostly ex-polo ponies inherited from a departing civilian, on condition that the ponies were not to be ridden by men. Now that she had been evacuated there was no one to supervise or exercise the animals. Soon, along with the Egyptian *syce**, I was running a riding club for the camp. In the pre-dawn light of those terrible Cairene days, two or three of us would set out cantering across the sand, flat as the eye could see, the countryside grey in the dawn, unbelievably colourless. Slowly the sky would turn pink and gold, and almost without warning a great fiery sun would flood the earth with colour; for a few magic minutes the sand would be golden, the distant hills blue, the palm trees in the scattered settlements green, the poverty-stricken kids nut brown; the distant roofs of Heliopolis red. Half an hour later, heat haze enveloped everything into a smudged tan colour, sweat would pour from us and our mounts. It was time to go back to cold fried eggs and over-brewed tea.

We had a number of adventures on those rides. One time, when passing a mini oasis settlement, the women in their long black garments suddenly realized we were also women despite our jodhpurs and invited us in. We accepted, dismounted, and sat on the sand holding our reins. We found it hard to refuse the food and drink they so

---

\* syce - Arabic & Hindu word for a man who looks after horses - a groom. Used throughout the East.

generously proffered, but we had to refuse it. Fly-covered excrement lay everywhere. Several times I fell off my light-footed pony on to the forgiving sand; once I lamed my pony and came back late. Then one day, while passing another settlement, we were surrounded by Arab men. They caught hold of my stirrup and tried to dismount me. I used my crop brutally to lash out; fortunately my lively little pony used his hooves to greater effect. We rode away, soon out of earshot of the rude shouts.

"There's no need to report this, now Topsy," I suggested to my companion, an Irish girl much senior to myself.

"No, I'm afraid I must!" she replied.

There was to be no more riding; I was not even to cross the desert alone on foot to the stables to supervise the ponies. The prison gate closed in further. But inside those prison walls something had happened. The whole atmosphere had changed. Everyone was more confident, less fearful that defeat was inevitable. It showed in the way people smartened up their uniforms, walked taller, smiled more, and it showed in the letters the men wrote home and which we had to censor in our off-time. I had done some of the cyphers appointing General Montgomery to be commander-in-chief, I had seen some of his communications with Prime Minister Churchill. I had listened to one of his pep talks, and I had blessed him for quickening the delivery of mail from Britain, but it took me months to connect all these improvements with the appointment of this one man.

I had still not acquired a boyfriend of my own. At TME the few men in the mess were mostly older men of the signals branch, who appealed to me as little as I to them. The camp was two miles from the Heliopolis tram terminus whence it took half an hour into Cairo, or ten minutes to the Heliopolis sports club. There was no transport to spare for a liberty bus. Once the riding was stopped I joined the sports club in Heliopolis and tried to swim as often as I could.

On one occasion members of the Mess were invited over to the villa of an important pasha who was known for his generosity and helpfulness to the British troops. Four of the younger WAAFs who were off duty that night were told to attend, and were briefed that we might be skilfully questioned. Part of our training had been to recognize probing questions, how to be tactful in answering them, and who to report to afterwards.

Now we were told to parry the questioners, and try to find out who they were, where they worked, and what they wanted to know.

We drove with a senior WAAF officer to a handsome villa set in an oasis of a garden between us and Cairo. Twenty or more sleek-looking Egyptian men were assembled, and two or three very handsome and elegant ladies. Except for ourselves there was no one under forty in the room. We were accorded a very warm welcome, with many compliments as to how beautiful we were and what a pity that we had to wear such dull uniforms and spend all our time doing secretarial work.

"You do secretarial work, of course?" asked a great fat slob of a man, handing me what I thought was the soft drink I had requested and leading me to a balcony overlooking the garden.

"Oh, I do anything that comes along!"

"What do you mean?"

"Well, you see, the more people you have, the more administration you have to keep them all paid and fed and clothed, and then the more people you need to do the administration, and so it goes. We know we are in for a very dull few years. But it's lovely to see Cairo! Tell me what you do. That must be far more interesting!"

He took my empty glass from me and told the waiter in Arabic to put in a double gin and fill it up with orange juice. Swahili is full of Arabic words, so I understood the gist of what he was saying. When the drink came back I took a tiny sip, and walked to the edge of the balcony, where there was a potted palm. I already felt woozy after the first drink, and was determined not to swallow any more.

"What a wonderful night. Do tell me, what star is that?" I asked. His eyes followed my pointing right hand as my left hand poured the drink into the palm tree. He kept trying to edge me towards the centre of the balcony again, under the light. It was only later that I realized the light was probably bugged.

"Have you been here long?"

"I came only because of the war. Have you always lived in Cairo?"

Two young men stood just inside the window, and while talking hard he summonsed them with the Arabic gesture that in other countries would mean 'Go away'. He introduced them to me, then took my empty glass and handed it to one of the young men, touching the Kenya flash I had on my shoulder:

"This young lady comes from Kenya and no doubt speaks Swahili so she understands Arabic." He was grinning as he watched for my reactions. I could not help but grin back. "She is drinking only orange juice, so would you fill her glass for her!" He added quietly in German: "*Etwas viel starker!*" (Something much stronger!)

So I had not outsmarted them. It was just his bad luck that he had picked the only WAAF there who understood both Arabic and German. The orange juice came back. I was desperately thirsty and sweating like anything in the humid evening air, and had no doubt consumed a double gin in my first drink without noticing it. I dared not drink any more. Now one young man was left alone with me; he was a great charmer and very knowledgeable about Egyptian antiquities. He offered to take me out on trips to all kinds of interesting places, but throughout our conversation he kept angling questions at me. In what circumstances would we be evacuated? where would we go? how many of us were there? what was my work? was I attached to a flying unit? were more flying units being sent out from Britain or America? And so on and on.

It was wearying work, parrying the questions, remembering what he wanted to know, longing for the drink I dared not touch.

"You are not drinking! Don't you like that orange juice?"

"I don't like vodka! It makes me talk too much, and I talk enough as it is!"

Asking once again for help in identifying the stars, I managed to glance at my watch. We had been there over an hour; I would find the others. I handed the full glass back to him and went to find the senior WAAF officer. She saw from my eyes that it was time to go and gathered up her party. On the way home we were debriefed. Three out of five women had been pressingly quizzed, all had had their soft drinks doctored. Later we were told that the villa had long been under suspicion, that it was in direct radio contact with the German forces, that four men were suspect spies whose activities had been confirmed by their questioning of us.

That evening as I lay in bed, I wondered at the timing of the party. Early in August I had seen cyphers telling of the appointment of one General Montgomery, who was to replace Alexander as Commander of the Eighth Army, the Army then holding Rommel from advancing into Cairo. Since then I had done the cyphers telling of his arrival, and had been told to attend one of the many pep talks he was giving all over Cairo. I had noticed with pleasure how much faster our mail was arriving from Britain. (I kept up a lively correspondence with old friends.) Even the airmen's outgoing letters which we had to censor in our off time were more cheerful. Our hosts that evening must have noticed the improvement too, and were trying to discover the reason.

Since we were one of the few women's messes left in Cairo, we received numbers of invitations from men's messes. Every free evening some dozen of us would climb into a swaying three-ton truck to be delivered to some other mess as dreary as our own, where we would dance, drink beer, watch an ENSA show, and flirt with complete strangers for a few hours before being driven back to our own sandy barracks.

It was on one of these mass blind dates that I met Peter. I had put my name down to go to a concert party at a mess only five miles away – 106 Equipment Unit. Nice and near, I thought, no long exhausting ride in a swaying three-tonner. Moreover, the entertainment was a variety show by professionals and reputedly very witty. Even Mrs Garston, the grandmother of A-Watch who never came to anything, had put her name down. Before the war she had been a keen amateur actress.

Peter, then a flight lieutenant, was on duty to meet and seat the visitors, and I was delighted when he sat next to me. I was drawn to him because he looked so like my father, although taller – he was a good six foot, he had the same high forehead lengthened by a widow's peak of golden hair, long thin features and laughing blue eyes. But he did not laugh at the ENSA jokes, he was too embarrassed. The ENSA group giving the concert had not realized that women would be present, so each joke was bluer than the one before. Peter started by apologizing, and as the show went on and the jokes grew bawdier, he kept glancing sideways at me, not meeting my eyes, cringing, speechless with embarrassment. The jokes were mostly childishly vulgar; I laughed even at those I did not understand because I would not admit to ignorance or prudishness.

"I cannot imagine a more unsuitable show for a young girl. You didn't really find that funny, did you?" he asked at the end as I sat clapping. Later I was to remember that he liked his women old-fashioned.

"No, but your embarrassment was!" I replied, "after all, one cannot be entirely ignorant and serving up here!"

He looked at me in surprise, and went off on his social duties. Soon he was at my side again, escorting me round the buffet table.

"You got off well with that dishy flight lieutenant!" Penny was sitting next to me on the way home. "When are you seeing him again?"

"He was totally embarrassed, poor man, at the blueness of the jokes. He didn't even ask me out. I expect he's married!"

"You mean you don't even know?" She sounded incredulous.

"He'll ask you out." It was Mrs Garston. "I know, I saw him look at you." Nobody argued with Mrs Garston; she said she was forty-eight and was probably older, a cheerful woman who kept her past to herself, worked well, and frequently covered up for my errors. She was a fount of information about Cairo, where she had lived for many years; and about life itself.

Mrs Garston was right, there was a note for me next day, and an invitation to go swimming and have lunch on Sunday. On Sunday I was on duty. Peter came to the mess for dinner when I came off duty in the evening. Future dates had to be planned for my complicated watch schedule.

"Ah!" said Mrs Garston, seeing us in a corner, heads together as we compared diaries. We made a date for one week ahead, but when the day came I received another note saying he had tonsillitis and was in hospital. Would I forgive him and postpone the outing for one week? He was out of hospital earlier than expected and came round to the mess for a drink before I went on watch. We had of course planned another date; this time it was my turn to delay. I deciphered it myself, the message that was to recall me home to Kenya.

We were already into September. By this time I had been promoted to the manic activity of the machine room. The cypher machine was a sort of very noisy typewriter with a drum on either side. Messages, usually written in pencil on signals paper, consisted of random letters in groups of five. Signals messengers placed piles of them in baskets according to priority, and from these we helped ourselves. For each message we adjusted the various settings on our machine, typed out the letters on the keyboard, and two long streamers of paper emerged, one from each drum. One strip carried the meaningless letters we had typed, the other the message. We trailed both strips to a central table and pasted the message tape onto a signal pad; the other tape we used only to check our typing if the message came out corrupt. I had picked this message because it came from Nairobi. Now the words seemed to tumble around me:

*"Inform A.S.O. Watkins Father very ill major operation planned Monday sixth September request return home immediately."* I pasted up the message and put it at the bottom of the pile, to hand in at the end of the watch. To finish this watch, I could bend over my machine in a haze of tears, and no one would notice. I did not want sympathy or I would break down altogether. I would speak privately to the officer of my watch, Joy, when we got back to the mess.

Ought I to go home? I had settled in well in the five months since I had left home. I felt I was doing a useful job here, part of a team; I would be deserting my friends. That very watch had revealed that Rommel was once again throwing everything he had got at the Eighth Army. It was by no means certain that they would be able to hold the positions they had occupied since June. Cairo was still in danger. Yet I was but a very small cog in the war machine and my presence at father's bedside might well be crucial to his recovery. I also knew that the decision would probably not be mine to make. Joy was all kindness and sympathy, and said I should go into Cairo to see Groupie.

In Cairo our Group Officer saw me at once. She too was extremely kind; and had already heard my news. She said although compassionate leave had been stopped for the entire Middle East, she had arranged for me a temporary posting to Nairobi. She would let me know about transport in a few days. A few days? I could not wait so long. I dashed round to my South African friend, Charles. The South Africans had lots of planes flying through Nairobi, where they had to stop to refuel. Charles picked up a telephone.

"Yes, she's an officer!" I heard him say. He told me there was a South African Lodestar leaving at dawn next day; they would be delighted to offer me a passage providing I would look after six other ranks of the South African Women's Auxiliary Air Service on their way back to South Africa.

"I'm only going to Nairobi!" I said.

"That will do nicely!" Charles replied firmly.

Back at the mess I hardly had time to pack my kit and put it in the storeroom. My flight officer eased my guilt at going by saying she already had a replacement for me; a girl who had been off sick for some weeks had returned to work. By the time I reached Almeira Airport the sky was grey with dawn, and the neat little Lodestar plane stood ready. Two groups of people all in the same uniform stood practising apartheid on the tarmac, men and women of the South African Air Force. I went over to the men; the most senior was the pilot, a major. I saluted him as smartly as I could, trying to conform to airforce custom.

"A.S.O. Watkins reporting for the flight to Nairobi, Sir."

He looked at me with impatience; there was distaste in his eyes as they went up and down my body, looking me over as if I were a head of livestock. He clearly did not approve of what he saw. I was discomforted by his silent hostility.

"That's your group, over there." He pointed to the women. I saluted again, and went over to them. They were all NCOs, pasty-faced, overweight, in their mid-twenties, substantially older than myself, and every one looked as if she had been weeping. They were too miserable to remember to salute me. I wondered what was wrong.

"Looking forward to going home?" I asked cheerfully.

"Oh no, ma'am," they chorused, and tears started to flow again. Before anyone could recover we were all loaded into the plane, each of us carrying our own luggage. The six South African women had a tremendous amount and no one helped us lift it into the luggage compartment. Even before we took off, two women grabbed paper bags and started being sick. The rest joined in as the plane rose above Almeira Airport and headed south. One of them passed me a paper bag.

"No thanks, I'll wait until it gets bumpy!" I laughed.

"When's yours arriving?"

"My what?"

"Your bybie, of course!" Her accent was so strong I found it hard to understand her.

"I'm not having one!" I replied indignantly.

"Then why are you going home?" she asked. When I told her, she started crying in sympathy. Six pregnant women, and I was responsible for them for the next forty-eight hours! Someone should have warned me. Fortunately I was too ignorant to know any of the many things that might have gone wrong.

I started thinking. It was the first time I had had time to think for months. What was life going to be like without Father? Why were our minds so alike, our reactions so much the same? Even so, I had not realized what it must have cost him when I joined up. I had thought of our parting as a temporary one that would end with the war. He already knew it was something more permanent, more lasting, but he never said a word.

# Chapter 4
## Lodestar to Kenya

The seats in the Lodestar were wonderfully comfortable, much better than those in the flying boat had been. I stretched my legs luxuriously. Although the South African girls were retching all round me, I had learned complete concentration on the job in hand. Now I could think about my father. Why *were* we so close?

It was partly due to the unusual circumstances of my family. My father, a senior colonial administrator, had retired when I was only nine years old and we had moved to England for the education of my sisters and myself. Father had taken on much of our upbringing during our school days, leaving Mother free to follow her many other interests: journalism, her coffee farm in Kenya, her mother in Austria, and her constant need to help others. Twice during my few years at school, I had to take a term off and rest most of the time because of a weak heart. It was my father who taught me, coaching me patiently so I won scholarships and passed exams. Our minds worked in the same way.

In 1938, after five years in England, my parents returned to Kenya leaving me at school I joined them soon after war was declared, and my father and I became closer than ever. My two older sisters wanted to join up, and I was told it was my turn to be farm help to Mother. Sixteen is the age when mothers are always wrong. I wanted to continue my studies, not become a farm girl. I was neither as patient nor as practical as my sister, Ronny, nor was my heart in the routine of farm life.

Next term I was sent as a weekly boarder to Limuru girls' school, only twenty miles up the corrugated earth road. Limuru was the only girls' school in Kenya to have a sixth form. What none of us had realized was that this particular sixth form offered needlework, singing, typing and English. I am tone deaf, hate sewing, and had already covered the ground and even the set books of the English course. The typing would be useful, but hardly justified the fees my father was paying. The head-mistress, Miss Fisher, the sister of the then Archbishop of Canterbury, was a formidable lady but then so was my mother. It never occurred to me not to confront her.

"I need French, Latin and History for Higher Certificate and University Entrance, and I would like mathematics too please!" I said crisply when she condescended to see me.

"No question of teachers being available during the war!" she replied.

On my first weekend in Nairobi I went to see the Reverend Roland Allen, a retired octogenarian missionary who had volunteered to coach me in Latin if ever I needed it. Now he offered to come up to the school if transport could be arranged. Father agreed to drive him, and to provide lessons in Ki-swahili and history. Neither wanted pay-ment, not even transport money if lessons could be arranged on Friday afternoons or Monday mornings when I had to be transported anyway. Both men made the same remark: "I shall regard it as part of my war work!" I returned to Miss Fisher in triumph. I had arranged two or three courses for the sixth form with no cost to the school. I thought she would be delighted.

"Men! Teaching up here, in a girls' school!" Her voice implied her horror at what an eighty-year-old missionary and my sixty-year-old fa-ther might do to her girls. On Father's next visit Miss Fisher summonsed him to tell him my heart was not in my work.

"What work?" I asked, when he handed on the comment. "She hasn't given me any!" I did not need to be reminded that I had asked for the opportunity to study, that the fees were high, that I was away from the irritations of the farm. Yet I knew that Father sympathised with me. Why else did he put up with my next escapade?

A few weekends later I borrowed my eldest sister's clothes and went into Nairobi on Saturday morning, where I spent my pocket money on powder, lipstick and hairpins. In the ladies' lavatory of the New Stanley Hotel I put into action the plan I had been rehearsing for weeks. I combed out my pigtail and arranged it in a bun at the back of my head – it added years to my age. I used lipstick and face powder for the first time in my life and fled through the back door of the hotel to avoid meeting friends. Up Harding Street, round the corner to the BMC building, up the stairs of the Meteorological office, along the passage to Mr. Walters' office.

Mr. Walters was an old friend of my father's, a round jolly little man of remarkable achievements. He had once been arrested by the police for letting off purple balloons near the post office, and taken to the local asylum. These were experimental meteorological balloons to measure wind currents. He wanted to see if they would work at Nairobi's high altitude. Somehow during the difficult years of the slump he had built up well-equipped statistical and meteorological departments for the government, covering the whole of East Africa. Once when we met him, Father had told him I wanted to read mathematics at university. He had turned to me and said, "Let me know when you want a job, I can always use mathematicians."

Now he received my unannounced visit courteously, offered me a chair, addressed me as Miss Watkins, listened to what I said.

"You have to be nineteen, you know, to work in a government department." He was cranking an old-fashioned telephone to summon one of his minions, and gave me no chance to reply. The minion was a tall, sallow young man who hid his shyness behind a huge moustache and an abrupt manner. He led me off and spent half an hour making me convert temperatures from Fahrenheit to Centigrade, pressures from pounds to kilos. It was hardly higher mathematics.

"I expect Mr. Walters will be in touch with you!" He released me into the passage. It was later than I had intended. In the lavatory I took down my hair and scrubbed the makeup from my face before going to meet Father. I met Mr. Walters first.

"Ah, now I recognize you better!" he grinned. I blushed and rushed past him, saying Father was waiting for me. What a fool I had been! Now he had seen how young I was there would be no hope.

Back at school, the days seemed endless, the boredom unendurable. Why had I left the farm? That was at least never dull. In an English newspaper I saw a recruitment advertisement for WAAFs and filled it in, lying about my age.

One morning when I came out of breakfast at school, Father's car was standing in the drive. At that moment Father appeared with Miss Fisher.

"What's happened, Dad?" I asked.

Miss Fisher looked down her nose. "Your efforts to obtain employment have borne fruit. Your father has come to fetch you. Get your things. Good luck to you!" Her voice conveyed 'good riddance'. I waited until I was in the car with my small amount of luggage, my Alsatian Sheba panting wetly over my shoulder.

"What happened, Dad?"

"It's just as well we got in first. She thinks you have too many ideas for your own good, or that of the other girls," he replied. "And now, young woman, if you take this job, you stick to it, do you understand? This is your third change in six months. The war is putting considerable strain on my generation. I'm not going to have my friends messed about by a discontented-sixteen-year-old. You need not take the job – the pay is £15 a month, the hours long and demanding. If you do take it, you stay at least one year."

"When do I start?" I was breathless with excitement. Of course I would take it.

"The first of the month, that's tomorrow. That's why I had to come up today!"

"Did Mr. Walters ring you up, Dad?" I asked nervously. I had not told him I had applied, nor what had been left unsaid over my age, nor about my application to the WAAFS. Suppose they accepted me and I wanted to change again?

"Yes! You might have warned us. He asked for Miss Watkins, and I called each of your sisters to the phone before we realized who had applied."

Fifteen pounds a month, it was a fortune for a girl in those days, three times the lowest pay of a typist or telephonist, as much as some farm managers earned; it was enough to run a car. Of course I would stick it.

On 1 March 1940 I started work, and almost at once the challenge came. We had to work at weekends, and Easter Weekend fell to my lot. The family assembled at home, only I had to go to work. Father drove me into work weeping and fetched me back no happier.

"It's too much for the child!" said Mother.

"Nonsense!" said Father. "We all have to learn to work. The younger, the better!"

Apart from working at weekends I enjoyed the job and enjoyed even more the wonderful feeling of being grown up and earning money. But I nearly came to grief. Four times a day maps had to be plotted neatly in two coloured inks, six items of information written in against each of about fifty stations, temperatures and pressures converted to the metric system. We had to use two colours, red and blue ink, and to do this had devised a system of splicing two wooden nib-holders together. Maureen, who was eighteen and showed me the ropes, was both quick and neat; it was because she was so good that I, another young girl, had been taken on.

I too was quick, particularly with figures, but neatness had never been my strong point. After a few weeks I was called in and given a warning. Some maps were illegible. If my work did not improve... My heart was in my mouth. How would I live it down at home, not accepted at school, sacked from my job? The next few weeks were harrowing; by the end of the month I was living on tenterhooks. The sacking never came, probably through no virtue of mine. Suddenly they needed me more than before.

In May the phoney war ended and real war began. When Italy joined Germany and declared war on Britain, Italian troops in Ethiopia advanced over the boundary into Kenya, making it one of the first British territories to be occupied by the enemy. Reinforcements poured into Kenya from South Africa, Rhodesia, Tanganyika, West Africa. The RAF establishment in Nairobi was strengthened by the South African Air Force. Overnight the meteorological office gained importance. Both the area and the frequency of observation were extended, we were all sworn to secrecy, even routine reports came in cypher, the office worked eighteen hours a day and our team of four workers was doubled to eight. Before my seventeenth birthday I had become one of the old hands.

We were a strange collection of women. There was the old settler who regaled us with stories of how she had married at the age of sixteen and wondered why she was growing so fat until her husband told her where babies came from. She had given birth to her first son alone in a mud hut while her husband was out on safari. Then there was a thirty-year-old grass widow who nearly committed bigamy unwittingly – her husband was reported missing believed dead in Ethiopia, but suddenly turned up eighteen months later, a few days before her wedding to a South African colonel. These two women discussed sex endlessly, ending each session: "All men are the same in their pyjamas."

There was also talk of air raids. Mother always believed in being prepared. To my acute embarrassment she arrived on the office doorstep one day and accosted the first person she met, the tall, thin young man who had interviewed me. We girls had nicknamed him Nunkie (short for Uncle) and teased him mercilessly.

*

For two years I kept doing my watches, plotting material from all over Africa, coding and decoding, working the telex to the wireless station. When I reached my seventeenth birthday, I took my driving test, and bought a discarded bull-nosed Austin 7 for £5. It looked like an aeroplane without wings, so I painted it in RAF colours, spent £15 on having it done up, and roared around Nairobi. Life was good; my job was interesting and I enjoyed living at home. I felt guilty not helping Mother more when she was working so hard – in 1941 she was elected to the Legislative Council to replace Lord Erroll, who had been the victim of the infamous murder summed up by the American headlines: *"Belted Earl Bumped Off by British Bart!"*

To assuage my guilt, I undertook all the chores I could in Nairobi, often doing all the household shopping and collecting the post. Also I looked after my father, seeing to his clothes and his diet, persuading him to take the injections of liver extract which kept him going. I helped him with his share of chores, looking after the oil lamps we used, making sure all the mechanical things about the place worked, that the clocks were wound and set, the cars serviced and cleaned. We shared transport to work when my hours permitted, often lunched together, exercised the dogs together, rode and played chess together. I liked the fact that I could walk about in his mind but was sometimes dismayed when he walked into mine.

The war retreated from East Africa. The pressure of work lessened. The grass widow left to join her husband, the old settler wife was superannuated, the neat and pretty Maureen walked up the aisle with one of the met officers, and I graduated to senior supervisor, on the princely salary of £25 a month. I recruited my friends to the office as they left school, interviewing the mothers as well as the daughters. It was time I moved on.

It was just before my eighteenth birthday when I happened on an advertisement in the local paper: "*Urgently needed, women to join the Royal Air Force and serve in the Middle East. Must be officer material. Age 25 to 35 Ability to type, quickness at figures, free of all ties.*" I felt in my pocket, where there was still the refusal of my third application to join the WAAFs. Was I officer material? Could I add seven years to my age? The Met office had accepted me as three years older than I was; but another four? I looked long and hard at myself in the mirror, and studied my eldest sister Pella carefully. She was twenty-three and I was often mistaken for her. I would give twenty-three a go.

Four weeks later I was summonsed to attend an interview at RAF Headquarters in Nairobi. There were one hundred and forty applicants, at the most twenty vacancies. I was not hopeful; and, with the given age of twenty-three, was sent away as being too young. By careful enquiry I discovered the next step was a medical at Eastleigh Airport. I turned up with the others (by now only fifty were left), apologizing that I had lost my piece of paper. The doctor was old, fat and had an expensive complexion.

"You are cutting your wisdom teeth a bit late, Miss Watkins, and what about that murmur in your heart?"

"Just a little trouble, years ago," I muttered. "I ride and play squash even at this altitude."

"Don't murmur, girl, it's bad enough when your heart murmurs. I gather they need you urgently, so I'm letting you through, but people in your category have to sign an indemnity paper, that there can be no claim on the service if the condition gets worse. Do you want to go on?"

"Yes." And then because he seemed such a kindly old man I asked: "Why do they want us so much?"

He stared at me a moment, the fat old doctor with a purple nose. It was a kindly face overlaid with sadness. He was not the only man, in the autumn of 1941, who feared we were losing the war. Pearl Harbour and the American reaction to it were still in the future.

"When Greece and Crete and Cyprus fell, and in every desert retreat, a batch of cypher officers has gone into the bag. They sent more out from Blighty, and both lots went down in the Atlantic. Now they're recruiting here. Sure you want to go on?" I knew he knew I was lying about my age, but he did not say anything.

Next day I turned up to headquarters bearing my soiled bill of health. There were only about thirty of us; we were all given a twenty-minute test, decyphering with a book code and then typing all capitals very quickly; both had been part of my life for two years. The testing went on for two-and-a-half hours. Long sight enabled me to read the tester's notepad upside down. I noticed I had gained top marks for both tests and also that they had checked us for security and again – thanks to my parents, who had no idea I was taking this test – I had a high rating.

I was full of confidence when I followed on into the interview room at their call of "Next Please". I hoped that they would not recognize me now I was wearing my second sister's clothes. There was no such luck.

"Didn't we tell you not to come back?" the squadron officer asked as I came in.

I moved firmly to the interview chair and sat down. At least I had had time to think what I should say. Mother used to pick up quotations she liked and overwork them. Now I borrowed one of her favourites, ironically straight from Mussolini.

"Youth is a disease from which we all grow better every day!" I announced firmly, looking the squadron officer straight in the eye. I was relieved to see surprise and amusement rather than annoyance. Glances were exchanged between the four officers, suppressed smiles, a slight nod. A new form was taken out to be filled in; my health papers were not even examined.

"We'll be in touch in about four weeks. Can you leave your present job by then?"

"Of course." No need to mention that it was a reserved occupation. I was in, I was about to become a WAAF, a member of the RAF, the most glamorous job in my war-stricken world. In high animal spirits, I hooted and tooted the horn of my little car eight miles all the way home. Now I would be able to get my own back for Mac.

Mac was the first man I had fallen in love with, at the age of just fifteen. In 1938, I had had to have another term off school and my parents had taken me out to Kenya. I travelled back alone on board ship, and four RAF pilots had joined the ship at Port Said. In those days even pilots travelled by sea. I had forgotten my determination to study and Mac and I had played games all day together and spent much of the night dancing and playing ping-pong. We had stood together on the ship's rails, watching the phosphorescence on a wonderful Mediterranean night and he had told me his story. He came from a poor background and, one day, in pouring rain and while on the way home from school, he had stopped to help a delivery man unload his truck full of clothes to a new Marks and Spencers store. The manager had been so impressed by him that he had offered him a job, and he had worked there for seven years, going quickly up the ladder, adding a year or two to his age here and there, and becoming a manager himself when only twenty-one, earning £1,000 a year – in those days a princely salary.

Even so, he decided shopkeeping was dull and had applied to the RAF for flying training, had taken a few mathematics lessons, and passed into the flying school. He had now, in 1938, completed his first tour of duty, and loved the life. The Women's Auxiliary service had just been restarted – why did I not apply to join up too? he asked.

"What do women do?"

"Oh, secretarial work, store-keeping, cooking, that sort of thing."

"Would you join a service to do that sort of thing?"

"You know I wouldn't, but you're a girl. We could ask for a posting to the same station and have some fun!"

"But I want to study!"

"Don't be too long. There's a war coming and when it does I won't last for more than six months."

"How do you know?"

"I just do!"

A month after we docked he was down at the school to take me out, armed with a big bunch of flowers. The school sent him away without telling me. I had not received his letters because they had forwarded them to my parents in Africa. I only discovered this at Christmas when I sent him a card, and he replied at once, to my holiday address. He was just going overseas on another posting. I never saw him again. He was wrong about the six months; he actually lasted one year, and died in the Battle of Britain. My letters had been returned to me. This was why I had to join the WAAFs, no other job would do.

Now that I had got into the airforce, I had to get out of my current job. My letter giving one month's notice was received with gratifying dismay. Nunkie told me I was banging my head against a brick wall. He could not join up, why should I? All the men stressed I was in a reserved occupation, doing splendid work; they were going to put my pay up to £30 a month, but they would not release me. Luckily Mr. Walters was away – he was a member of the Manpower board before whom my release would have to go. My father too was a member of the board.

"It wouldn't be right for me to attend the board when your application is heard," he said, "but I'll help you write a letter to them!"

"Now I'm at last eighteen I should surely be allowed to serve my country in the service of my choice," he wrote. "My present job could well be done by someone not so young as I am, and not free to travel." I was afraid that the RAF might see this letter and my real age would be revealed, but I did not want to tell my father I had lied about my age.

He knew his colleagues and I was released. When he brought the news home, he took me into the garden and showed me a Biretta pistol, a small and compact automatic weapon in a neat leather case. There were two complete magazines of ammunition, each with six bullets. He pinned a homemade target against a tree.

"One of the young soldiers who used to come here gave me this. He liberated it in Ethiopia. He said one of you girls might one day need it. I'm going to show you how to use it." After a few shots, when I managed to hit the target, he unloaded the gun and showed me how to test that it was empty.

"You may be the holder of secret information. In that case don't let the Germans capture you. If it looks likely, this is the place to shoot." He held the emptied gun first against his head, then mine.

"Of course, I'd rather you didn't, but the choice must be yours. I shall understand." He looked at me again, love shining from his eyes. "You'll certainly never get through the war without men trying things on. If you are attacked this is the way to deal with it." He sprang on me, and brought me to the ground. Then he showed me how to free my hands to press on eyeballs, my knees to kick on other balls.

"Never let a man you don't want get nearer than this!" he demonstrated.

"And what if I do want?" It was an idle question, to lighten a grim demonstration. The answer was not light.

"If you feel your heart would break if you refused and he were to be killed, then go ahead. If in doubt, say no. And if anything happens, remember that's what fathers are for!"

"But what would you do, if I had an illegitimate child?" I was so surprised that I had to spell it out, in case I had misunderstood him. There was no pill in those days, I had never heard of condoms. I thought of the church, the gossip, the shame it would bring him.

"I would take a nice little holiday in South Africa. You, my dear, would accompany me. Only when the child was born would we decide what to do about it. Most mothers seem to want to keep the little nuisances." He smiled at me, himself endeavouring now to keep the discussion light. He had clearly considered what might happen to his daughters in times of change.

At least this time I was not returning home for that reason – unlike my companions, I thought smugly, as I looked round the plane. The girls sat, puffy and dishevelled, like so many lumps of dough. I took out my comb and powder puff.

In 1942 passengers still did not fly at night. We had flown that day for twelve hours, coming down twice to refuel. Now, with sun low in the sky, we were landing at an RAF posting station in the midst of the scrub of the Southern Sudan. We walked across the sand towards the ugly cement buildings, the women stumbling along behind the men, clutching their bags. As I reached the mess, the pilot was waiting for me.

"You can't come in here!" he said. "It's an officers' mess, women not allowed!"

"Then where do we go, sir?"

"That's not my business. You're the woman officer, aren't you?" Did he always address women with that note of exasperation in his voice? It stung me into a rude reply:

"I see, we just stand here then, sir?"

He glared at me, went in and slammed the door. I opened the door to follow; he turned and pushed me out. I thought for a moment, went round to the back of the building, and found the mess sergeant.

"Crikey, what are you doing here, miss?" he asked as I walked in to his well-lighted storeroom from the African dusk. I explained my dilemma.

"I'll tell the CO, miss, he's in the mess."

A few moments later a boyish-looking group captain came out by the back door. He was not the least disconcerted by seven women dropping in on him.

"All officers?" he asked.

"No sir, I'm the only officer, the others are South African NCOs. I wondered if your personnel officer could help us?"

"Sergeant, have you eaten yet?"

"No, sir."

"Do you think you could rustle up food for six women sergeants, and be host to them? In our anteroom?"

The sergeant grinned. "With pleasure, sir! Would it be in order if I bring some of my mates over?"

"A very good idea, Sergeant. The hospital tents are empty at the moment. Put a big 'Ladies' sign on the nearest ablutions. Afterwards show the girls down there. The MO is in the mess. I'll have a word."

The CO and the sergeant walked me round the mess building as we talked. The women stood dejected, their bags on the sand beside them.

"They'd better go in there, sir!" The sergeant pointed at the officers' loo. The group captain nodded, the sergeant went in to make sure no men were inside; silently we all trooped in. Both men were waiting when we came out. It was a routine with which I was to become very familiar, dropping in and out of men-only messes.

The sergeant led the women off. The group captain turned to me. His badges and decorations told me flying type, almost certainly a survivor of the Battle of Britain and the desert campaigns.

"You'll be my guest for supper, of course?" he asked. "This is a great occasion, our very first WAAF officer." He held the mess room door open for me. The South African pilot was sitting at the bar watching the door. He was down from his stool and halfway across to evict me before he realized I was accompanied by an officer senior to himself. He looked nonplussed as the group captain stepped quickly in front of me and held out his hand.

"Glad to welcome you, Major. I believe you were kind enough to bring one of our officers with you, so you already know her!" He led me past the South African crew to the mess room and the veranda beyond.

"Do you often meet trouble like that?" he asked. The bar steward had followed him with cold drinks.

"Quite often," I replied, "but rarely from the RAF." I sensed a tenseness, a sadness about him.

"That's because we owe you girls too much! Were you a plotter, in 1940?"

Nineteen-forty was, of course, the year of the Battle of Britain, and plotters had plotted the dog-fights in the air. We sat there looking at the African dusk, at the great stars appearing in the flawless sky. In silence, I tried to share his memories. Suddenly the whole story poured out: the frenetic activity of those months; the sorrow of losing friend after friend, and then a much-loved WAAF killed by a bomb on the home station while he was in the air; the renewed vigour with which he had fought back; the emptiness of the ensuing decorations and promotion.

That night, sharing a hospital tent with the South African girls, I cried myself to sleep at the pain I had caused him, by being there, by wearing the same uniform as the dead girl. Usually when someone was killed in the RAF, his name was never mentioned again, but a man who was grieving would often talk to a woman. It was the first of many tragic vignettes shared with a complete stranger, the need to talk of the hurt.

At dawn breakfast the South African pilot was still glowering at me. He did not glower any less when the mess sergeant handed round the mess bills, putting one beside every plate but mine.

"The girls all right?" I asked him as he passed.

"Nothing wrong with their appetites, miss!" He rubbed his stomach. "I've cut sandwiches for you all!"

"Thank you, sergeant, and thank you for looking after them. Make sure we have plenty of paper bags, will you?"

"Paper bags? Of course, miss." He winked at me and was gone.

Eight hours later the Lodestar put down on Eastleigh Airstrip in Nairobi. My father, ashen-faced and thin, was on the tarmac to meet me. Courteous as always, he went to thank the pilot.

"Well, you've certainly got your troubles back with you!" the pilot said curtly, turning away.

"What's bitten him?" Father asked as I threw my bag into the back of the car.

"Me!" I told him the story. It was the only thing he laughed at all the way home.

# Chapter 5
## Nairobi

There is a long, straight, dull road leading from Eastleigh Airport. It was then called Watkins Road, after Father, because it was where he had had his headquarters camp for the Carriers in the First World War. On one side stood an estate of neatly placed little one-storey houses still gleaming new in September 1942. These had been the result of my mother's first venture into public works. Better municipal housing had been one of the planks of her platform when she was elected to the Municipal Council in 1921 and again when elected to the Legislative Council of Kenya in 1942.

Normally we made jokes about Olgaville developing on Watkins Road, but today there were no jokes. We drove down the main road towards Kiambu for a mile or two and then bumped off through the forest. It was all luxuriantly green, one of the last patches of virgin forest left around Nairobi. I reminded Father of my driving lessons along these tracks two years earlier, but all he said was that he felt such a nuisance, being ill, calling me back. It was Saturday afternoon. The operation on his stomach was scheduled for the following Monday. He would go into hospital tomorrow, Sunday. It was obvious that he did not expect to come through.

The road swept across the muddy Karura River, on to the farm and climbed the red earth track under a blaze of jacaranda trees. Wispers, our red brick farmhouse, was aflame with the deep orange of golden shower and the mauve blue of the potato creeper, the lawns were green and trim, the big shrubbery was gaudy with white frangipani, red poinsettia and hibiscus, blue plumbago – a mass of bright colours. Berries on the heavily-laden coffee trees were just beginning to turn red. The coffee-picking season would be early this year.

A pack of dogs converged on the car and my sister Ronny came out to meet us. She was by now vastly pregnant. I had not thought of my own sister looking like that. For some reason I burst into tears. To my dismay, so did she.

"I won't have you girls crying over your father! You know how he hates it!" My mother came out to greet me, giving me an enormous hug as she told me off.

"I'm not crying over Dad, I'm crying over Sheba; she's so delighted to see me!" I insisted. And certainly Sheba, my Alsatian bitch, was giving me an ecstatic welcome, yelping short shrill barks and jumping high into the air, springing round and round in circles.

"You look as if you could do with a bath." Mother looked at me critically. "We've heated the water specially."

This indeed was a great honour, offered to make guests feel very welcome, after a night in the train or days on safari. Bath water came direct from the river, by courtesy of a water-driven pump called a ram if it was working – otherwise on the back of Jackie, the donkey. It took two five-gallon tins of water to have a bath, and Jackie only carried two at a time. The water was poured by hand into a drum just outside the bathroom, heated by a wood fire, and piped through the wall. Hot baths were a luxury, rationed in number, usually taken in the evening before supper. The water was red and muddy in the wet weather and at coffee-picking time it stank of rotting coffee pulp.

After the bath I borrowed a car and reported to RAF headquarters. I felt triumphant driving into the place where I had been interviewed a year earlier, the sentry saluting me as he raised the barrier. There was an Australian flight officer in charge at the cypher office. She knew I was coming and had counted on me to start work that same evening. I learned later that it was her turn for duty but she wanted to go out with a certain group captain at whom she had set her cap. I was not amenable to extra duties. I had travelled much more quickly than usual by my own initiative and was on a compassionate posting. This was the one evening I could spend with my father. It was agreed, reluctantly on her part, that I should have the evening off but would go on duty the following afternoon, Sunday, as well as take on the long night session from 10 p.m. until Monday morning.

So far in the WAAF I had met courteous, friendly people and had worked well with my team. Kiwi was to prove the one exception in a long war. From that moment she had it in for me.

As a family, we had our evening together. We tried to make it a cheerful one, with Ronny and I capping each other's stories about our adventures in the services. She had left a similar job in the FANYS earlier that year. Next day, a Sunday, we all went to the Communion Service my father loved at the church he had helped found twenty years earlier, and then again to Matins, where he read the lessons. How well he read them, and how dear he looked with his white hair curling thickly from his high forehead, his blue eyes with the strange blue ring round the pupils, his grey suit hanging loose on his too-thin body.

Afterwards all the family dropped me at the WAAF mess, a long low wooden hutment in the grounds of the European primary school. There were lots of jokes about a primary school being the right place for me, and about the little cubicle allocated to me being smaller than Sheba's kennel at home – how would we both fit in? – for of course Sheba was accompanying me. There were only about eight of us in the mess, an ideal number for happy living, I thought, as I unpacked quickly and went into lunch.

The afternoon watch was surprisingly busy for a Sunday, all incoming messages. Various senior officers called in to see if there was anything of interest and, finding a new girl on duty, stayed to talk. Sheba was a great success, greeting everyone with a huge smile and an extended paw. She was a beautiful dog, short glossy black hair with a tan face and ears, tan markings on her chest, and tan front paws which she offered to anyone who noticed her.

Back at the mess I gulped down some supper, changed into my blue uniform, and did my hair with care. My father loved to see us all looking our best. As I was fastening Sheba's lead for the walk to the Maia Carberry Nursing Home, Kiwi came in. Her date had broken on her.

"All dressed up to go out, and you're on duty at ten!"

I was to become impervious to her harsh Australian twang with its aggressive sneer, but that evening I was vulnerable and tears sprang to my eyes.

"I'm going to see my father, then straight on to HQ, Ma'am. The nursing home is quite near!" I pulled my cap on as I spoke.

"Oh ya, who ever heard of visiting a nursing home all dressed up, and so late!"

"Good night, Ma'am, I won't be late for duty!" I grasped Sheba's lead in my left hand so I could salute with the right and walked off into the night.

Father was sitting up in bed. He looked comfortable and well cared for. There were flowers everywhere. Portrait photos of all of us stood on his bedside table with his favourite one of Mother. When it was time to say goodbye his voice broke and tears streamed down his face. I had never seen a man cry before. I could not look at him. At that moment the night sister came back again. She had a needle of something to give him, so I hugged him and went out into the dark.

"Don't forget," he called, his voice still slightly quavery, "it's our Silver Wedding tomorrow. Your mother's present is in that cupboard…"

Sheba was waiting for me; it was 9.15 p.m. I stood outside Father's window for ten minutes, looking in. He settled well, his spectacles on, his book open at the bookmark, his eyes already closed. I wondered if I would see him again, and allowed myself a few minutes to weep.

It was less than a mile to headquarters, so I arrived early and signed in with a steady hand. Mouse, who had taken over from me only a few hours earlier, fetched tea for us while she waited for transport. She was a slender girl with a sad little face, the sort of person you think you are helping when all the time she is helping you. She had been on A-Watch when I arrived in Cairo and hers was the first wedding I had been to after I arrived. Now she was a widow, sent to Nairobi to recuperate.

"What do we do when there's no work?" I asked as I looked at the empty baskets. The log book showed that it had been a busy afternoon for a Sunday but now the traffic had fallen off.

"You sleep, Nairobi, you sleep!" She helped me get the camp bed out, showing me the hook for the mosquito net.

"Is Kiwi always so disagreeable?" I asked.

"Yes, she was furious with you about last night. You'll have to be careful now, she likes to get her own back!"

It was quiet in the office. I waited for the duty officer to make his midnight call and blessed him for being early. Sheba and I climbed inside the mosquito net; the bed was against the wall and Sheba did her usual trick of putting her back against mine and pushing with her paws against the wall to make me move over. I had never shared a camp bed with her before, and when the bed turned over, depositing me on the floor with her on top of me, I decided I never would again... I had not succeeded in persuading her to accept this decision when there was a knock at the door.

"Hallo, miss, you're new here. Don't know what's happened up north, things hotting up!" A cheerful young signalsman who looked even younger than me placed a large pile of signals on the desk, many of them in the 'Immediate' basket:.

"Like some char, miss? Looks as if we are going to be busy!"

Ten minutes later he was back with an over-brewed mug, and another pile of 'immediate' messages. On his third visit I asked him to call the duty officer, who came in stretching.

"Why do flaps always occur when I'm on duty?" he grumbled. He took up the basket of decyphered messages and went to another desk. "God Almighty, what is going on in Egypt? Better get the CO."

The air commodore was away. The acting CO was the man Kiwi was chasing, a tall stringy group captain in slacks and pullover. I was typing furiously at my machine and he said, "I know you're the new girl, don't stop – you're doing a fine job." For some minutes he stood behind me watching the tape pour out of the machine, then he moved over to the camp bed, propped himself against the wall and put his feet up. Sheba edged up the bed and put her head on his knee. The duty officer was acting as my assistant, keeping the entry book, pasting up the long streamers of tape as they came out of the machine, handing the messages to the group captain. The signalsman brought another round of strong and bitter char and another batch of messages.

After an hour or so the men went off. I hammered the machine throughout the night. Gradually a picture emerged. The week-long German attack on British forces in the desert 40 km from Alexandria had been repulsed; Rommel's headlong sweep across the desert had been held. The Eighth Army had stood firm. Egypt was now less likely to fall than at any time in the last four months. As a result, redeployment was now happening, and its ripples spread down from the Middle East Command into the East African one. I wondered what the night had been like in TME; A-Watch would be on duty. No doubt it had been doubled up by combing the barracks for anyone sleeping.

Sheba snored contentedly now she had the camp bed to herself, occasionally giving little squeals in her dreams. The signals messenger brought more signals and more tea. I turned Sheba off the bed before the day watch came on duty at 7.45 a.m. She looked at me reproachfully and then came to sit beside me, one paw on my knee. Kiwi strode in and looked round the littered room distastefully.

"You shouldn't sleep, when there's work to do!"

"Have a heart," said Mouse, who was signing on in the log-book. "Six pages of entries since I went off last night, and the basket's nearly empty. She can't have slept at all!"

"I didn't! Mouse and I haven't looked at the corruptions – they're over there." There were always some messages we could not decypher.

"Then it's most untidy to leave the bed out! What will the men think?"

I did not tell her that the acting CO had spent an hour or more sharing it with Sheba, watching history come out of the machine, hoping as we all hoped that this was the turning point of the war. We thought it was the battle of Alamein, whereas in fact it was only the battle that made Alamein possible.

I left the office thankfully and went to register Sheba, as the duty officer had told me I must do.

"What breed?" It was a warrant officer who took the details.

"Alsatian."

"What sex?"

"Bitch."

"My God, what a country, even the dogs are bitches…"

Yet this was the one dog who redeemed the name of bitch. She adored my sister's Alsatian Solomon and would have only him. When taken to other dogs, she bit them where no lady should bite, and sat firmly on her tail. As soon as she was returned home she made for Solomon. It was his puppies she had.

Suddenly the personal import of the new day dawned. I decided not to go back to the mess. The headquarters building was a peacetime hotel and I found a bathroom and had a cold wash, then went to the canteen for yet another cup of tea and a sticky bun which Sheba and I shared. At the nursing home, Father was in the operating theatre and Mother was waiting in his room. I carried a chair into the garden for her and stretched out on the grass beside her.

Sleep did not come. I kept thinking about the work that night, somehow the signals had been different, more confident. When I thought about it I realized the atmosphere had changed before I left Cairo, when that strange new commander, Monty, had taken over. During 1942, England was being constantly bombed. At the same time the first waves of American soldiers were arriving there. Both these facts filled British troops overseas with dismay. If their children were not being blown to bits, what were their wives doing with those over-sexed, over-paid, over-there men? However many letters were faithfully written, few arrived, and those that did came in the wrong order. The Middle East was a giant sea of men miserable with worry about their families. Monty had sensed this, and had done something about it. Airmail letters were hastened on their way, aerograms and micrograms were introduced. Suddenly every man heard from home; life was liveable; there was something to die for.

At about twelve the surgeon joined us in the garden. He said Father was back in his room; that he had removed three quarters of his stomach, and did not know whether he would live or not. He insisted the growth was not malignant, but with so little stomach left, Father would be delicate for the rest of his life. I left Mother still questioning the doctor and retired to the broom cupboard to weep as I had never wept before. I do not know how long I stayed there. After a while I took out pen and paper and poured out my heart to Peter. Later I posted it, one of the most foolish things I ever did.

Presently Mother leant against the outside of the door, saying, "Don't take it so hard, don't take it so hard!"

The mess, the nursing home, and the RAF headquarters made up a triangle, which I walked and re-walked all that week, my faithful Sheba tugging me along. I called in twice at the nursing home between every stint on duty, sitting by Father, holding his hand, trying to doze when he did. On the third day he was sitting up in bed, his colour was better; hope returned.

Moreover, there were now other patients to visit. Ronny produced a fine baby son, the spit image of his grandfather, in another wing of the same nursing home. This was the first grandchild so the excitement was intense. The family trotted happily up and down the long corridor between the patients, and soon they were visiting each other. For my generation of the family it was our first near-confrontation with death, our first with new life. To have the two dramas running parallel in that one long, low nursing home against the background of working all night on messages about desert warfare was a heady amalgam.

I had now served six months and leave was due to me. Mother asked me to accompany Father to the Outspan Hotel at Nyeri for a week. The hotel lies high in the green country of Nyeri, with wonderful views towards Mount Kenya. The owner's wife, Lady Betty Walker, was a keen gardener and Father delighted in the wonderful gardens she had created. My heart and mind were no longer satisfied by playing chess, reading, eating huge meals, listening to Father comment ruefully that the first time in his life he had been able to afford a good hotel, he had literally no stomach for it. My restlessness did not go unobserved.

"Do you want to go back to the Middle East?"

"Yes," I replied, "of course, the action is there!" I could not tell him that I did not know the code word for the new offensive about to take place in North Africa. I could not tell him even about code words. I did not want to tell him about Peter.

"Then try to arrange it, and next time when your mother cables, don't come. I have to die some time, I don't expect you to ruin your career on it."

I waited until Father was working on his newspaper again, Ronny was at home and cooking for him. The family had settled down to life with a delicate and much cherished father, and a wonderful, even more cherished new edition. My posting was only temporary, and my request to return to the Middle East was readily granted. I wanted to be back before the New Year, when Peter was to go on a course in Palestine and would take leave before it, but for weeks every seat on every plane seemed booked. Then I was offered a seat to Khartoum on December 23rd. Nobody wanted a halfway ticket on that particular date. Father drove me to the airport at dawn.

"I'll always remember this day," he said, "it's my sixty-fifth birthday."

It was the first time in my life that I had forgotten it. I did not have a present for him. I had much to regret as the plane took off from Nairobi. And much to look forward to – at least so I thought. It was of course foolish to leave home so soon before Christmas, but I was triumphant. I would be in time to see Peter before he went off, and perhaps get a few days' leave to join him. He had written to me at least half a dozen times in twelve weeks. He must love me.

# Chapter 6
## Pursuit to Palestine

Khartoum had changed completely since my visit there nine months earlier. It was no longer a sleepy stop on a forgotten air route, but had become the crossroads of the Commonwealth. If you wanted to get from Bombay to London or New York, or from Canada to the war in the Indian Ocean, and you had enough brass on your shoulders and gold lace on your hat to score air travel points, you had to come through this unlikely spot. All aircraft, all airborne supplies, and most senior officers for both the Middle and the Far East were routed through Khartoum. The airport lay to the South, in the midst of desert. Even so, WAAFs were not usual items of cargo. Ordinary troops, junior officers and other ranks, men and women, took the eight-week sea journey from Britain round the Cape and all the way up to Suez. So when I walked into the officers' mess at Khartoum on Christmas Eve, the mess sergeant went to tell the CO there was a WAAF officer

The CO was having his bath, and he replied through the door: "I know it's Christmas, but pull the other one!"

It was dusk when he came down to greet me, the lights were not on, and he thought that I was one of the junior officers dressed up as a joke.

"Go and take that silly transvestite disguise off and come and join me for a drink, Johnson. It's not Christmas until tomorrow!" The voice was parental, irritated parent to tiresome child.

I did not know what transvestite meant and was somewhat taken back by this greeting but replied, "I am Section Officer Watkins in

**48**

transit to Cairo, and I'm not sure you would approve if I did so, sir! I have nothing else to put on!"

When he heard my voice, he blushed so scarlet I could see, even in the dim light. "I am so sorry, section officer, I really thought it was young James rehearsing for tomorrow. You're the first WAAF officer to visit us, and very welcome indeed. The VIP guest room is empty and you shall have it."

This was a great honour; there was a bleak row of hutments some yards across the sand for other transient officers, the mess sergeant had pointed it out to me. And I would not mind betting that the bathroom had no lock and the loos no doors. Now I had a comfortable room with its own bathroom – treasure indeed in the middle of a desert.

On Christmas morning the plane which had brought me from Nairobi departed for Takoradi and England. I had to find another to take me to Cairo. There were no other flights on Christmas day; and I was pressed into serving Christmas dinner to the airmen, a traditional part of Christmas day celebrations. These too were disinclined to believe that there could be a real WAAF about, and seemed convinced that I was a male officer dressed up. They laughed uproariously when I appeared, and punched me cheerfully in the chest, with such remarks as:

"Bloody marvellous get up, sir! Don't know 'ow you do it."

The day started at nine o'clock with an outdoor church parade for the entire station, all standing hatless as the sun beat down on us, most of them no doubt thinking of the cheerlessness of Christmas at home, their womenfolk trying to make something of the festival despite absent fathers and sons, eking out the scanty rations. Mine was the only head covered, the only one wondering what oddballs my mother had collected this year in that red-brick farmhouse I called home.

The day proceeded with all its silly pastimes, like balancing on a greased pole across the swimming pool. It dragged on for ever. I laughed a lot because everyone else laughed. I did not feel like laughing and I am sure no one else did either, but you cannot let a hundred or so men gloom their way through Christmas.

Then a pop approached me. "Pops" were older men, often wearing the ribbons of a previous war, and many had been slotted into cyphers, old duffers security-sound and able to handle cypher books. But now that books were being overtaken by machines, some of these older men were finding it difficult to keep up with the new technology. This pop asked me to look at his machine as it would no longer function and he had a pile of cyphers awaiting decyphering. We went up to the cypher office, and I tried the machine, which did not respond. I went to remove the drums; they cascaded sand all over the place.

"Had a sand storm recently?" I asked.

"Er, yes, early morning, day before yesterday. I didn't realize that sand had got in there!" He produced a cloth and we set to polishing the drums; then we each took one side of the heavy machine and turned it upside down, shaking hard, and more sand cascaded out. After we had cleaned it out, it worked beautifully. He sat down to test it, using two fingers and seeking out each letter.

"Why not let me do it, I touch type," I offered.

"You don't want to spend Christmas day doing my backlog of cyphers!"

"It'll be a pleasant change – I've lost count of the number of times I've been hit in the chest this morning and told how like a woman I look!" I was looking at the uncyphered messages. "Most of them seem to originate from TME. "If you want to get back to your duties with the games, I'll finish these off. Call me before they serve lunch –I'd better be seen helping there!"

I had a lovely quiet hour in an office by myself, working through a pile of cyphers. Then I noticed an English newspaper hidden away in the safe. Treasure of treasures, no wonder he had locked it up, it was less than a month old. I sat down for a good read. He came back at about 12.30.

"You mean, you've finished them all?" He was looking at the laden out-baskets, each labelled according to four grades of confidentiality and four of secrecy. Only the most immediate and top-secret baskets were empty. "That was a day's work for me. Come and let me buy you a drink!"

In fact, we went to help serve the airmen's dinner; ours was served in the mess in the evening. I was much honoured in that I had to cut the Christmas cake and make a speech, as I was the first WAAF officer to stay there. Everyone was expecting an entertaining performance from me, and I felt I was letting them down when, crimson with embarrassment and unhappiness, I said simply, "Thank you for having me." Then before I sat down I had a brainwave. In a more confident and cheerful voice, I managed: "And now, since so many of you" – I looked firmly at the CO on my left – "have mistaken me for young James Johnson, my double is going to stand in for me!" He handled the situation far better than I could have, telling a series of funny stories. Who minded if they were Pilot Officer Prune's mistakes, the fictitious character who always got everything wrong?

On Boxing Day only the air control officer and a pilot were down early. We three went out to the air control tower soon after dawn. It seemed a long wait before the first plane was ready to leave, a Blenheim on its way back from a major overhaul in Blighty. I sat in the back in the gunner's seat. If I lay on my tummy there was a marvellous view of the desert receding behind us, the green line of the Nile looping out of sight. But it is not easy to lie on your tummy in a tight skirt with a parachute clamped firmly between your legs. The noise was deafening and the vibrations seemed to be shaking my bones apart.

I fished in my bag for a fat book of short stories and read until I was brought back to the Blenheim flying down the Nile by terrible cramp in my legs. We were flying low, the sun was low on the horizon and seemed to shine through the sand, showing the skeleton of the burnt out land, where long ago rivers ran, and where the flood plains grew wheat. The pyramids came into view, the sun to the west of them casting huge shadows. The river stretched, green-bordered, behind us, and I contemplated that I did not even know at which airport we would arrive.

From the gunner's eyrie in the tail, the Helwan Airstrip rushed up to hit us with a thud. Trailing the parachute from the shoulder harness, I followed the pilot out of the plane, laughing at the astonished faces of the ground crew as a WAAF popped up from the gunner's retreat. I was overwhelmed with a sense of wellbeing by the fresh air of a Cairene winter. I had arrived, I would see Peter.

On the other side of Cairo, TME's grim barracks, were disappearing into the dark. With the black-out still in force, there was no light to be seen. There was a parcel and a letter waiting for me, both from Peter. I opened them with great excitement – only to discover they had been sent in September just after I left. I rushed to the phone, where it took me half a dozen calls spread over an hour to get any sense from his unit, which was in the process of moving west into the desert. Everyone was too security conscious to tell a strange voice on a telephone that they were moving, but they were happy to say that Peter had already left for Haifa to attend the staff officers' course, which started immediately after the New Year. He was taking a few days' leave and nobody knew where he was. This was the leave we had planned to spend together.

Disappointment must have been written all over my face. At that moment A-Watch came off duty and welcomed me warmly, thinking I was miserable about leaving home over Christmas. Of course I would be going back to them, no question of me joining another watch. I had supper with them, caught up with the gossip, was ready for duty early next morning. The air-conditioning had not arrived and conditions underground were still fuggy but in winter it was possible to come up into fresh air, cool and invigorating.

The work was as heavy as ever, and I had to concentrate to re-establish myself for long hectic sessions in the machine room. Working in the hole was causing much sickness, and there was a diphtheria epidemic going around. This was the time that I too started to be ill, much troubled by dysentery, vomiting and retching with every attack

One officer of my watch had a boyfriend, a young signals officer who worked underground with us, and he died of diphtheria. His funeral was my first in the RAF. Very often there was no funeral, for there was no body to bury. For this one we all paraded slowly to the cemetery, where the ceremony proceeded with full military honours and WAAFs sobbed round his grave. For the next six months hardly a week passed when I did not return to that cemetery and watch another cross added to the long rows.

One test pilot who had often taken me up crashed while he was testing a Blenheim, and after the funeral I sat down to write to his mother. Fortunately I mentioned this to another friend, Tom Deck. Tom was also a test pilot, his parents were from Kenya; and we had known each other all our lives.

"Don't be a fool, June, you can't possibly write!"

"Why not?"

He looked at me in dismay. "Didn't you know, he was married?"

Certainly the dead man had never mentioned it, fumbling at me in a taxi, holding my hand all the time. Personally I felt safe holding a man's hands – at least I knew where they were. Thank goodness I had repulsed his advances. Overall my conscience was clear, but should I have accepted the flights, the casual drinks, the odd evening out? In future I would be more careful. I was far too idealistic to want to become the other woman.

Tom Deck was back at Heliopolis Maintenance Unit as a test pilot after an extraordinary escapade, surely the original for "I am not waving but drowning"! He had been posted to a bomber squadron, and on one sortie was strafing German shipping off the coast of Turkey. He flew too low, damaged a wing on a mast, and had to ditch his plane off the Turkish coast. All the crew had their life-belts on and got out safely but the plane sank so quickly they did not manage to get the dinghy afloat. They were in sight of land, could see the sea wall quite clearly so it was not too difficult to swim for it. It was evening, the time when all the population promenade along the sea wall. Crowds gathered to watch the swimmers.

Tom had dislocated his shoulder and was by now in great pain. All three were desperately tired, the sea was cold, and they waved, hoping to be rescued. The onlookers waved back. They went on swimming until they could see every detail of the crowds watching, and again started waving. This time more people saw them and waved back. No one thought of coming to help. Not until they were staggering out of the water did anyone come forward. It was two policemen to arrest them. Tom cried out at the rough treatment of his damaged shoulder as they were all led away to an internment camp. I heard only that he had gone missing.

I think it was during Friday's prayers that, some weeks later, the two of them took the chance to escape, helped themselves to women's robes and at night managed to steal a fishing boat and set sail for Beirut. One evening the phone rang in TME and Tom was asking me down to drink to his return. He looked better than he had for a long time; no drink had been available in the camp, no parties, and no stress of frequent missions.

Tom often took me up when test flying, although this was forbidden. One day I sat perched beside him on a folding iron seat while he put a Wellington through its paces. I was observing his every movement, yet aware that the layout of the plane was such that the observer sat directly beneath us and kept looking up the iron bar, also observing everything. I always put on my glamour killers when I had to wear a parachute, but modesty had been so drilled into us that it still made me feel uncomfortable. Once I saw everyone smirking as I went out to the plane and wondered what was wrong; was I showing too much leg? Only when I took the parachute off did I see the owner's name, "Virgin", stamped right across it.

It was on this occasion that the pleasure of illicit flying came to an end, for the iron perch was not properly fastened. When the time came to get out of the plane, I dropped down into the nose as usual, and from there to the ground. The seat dropped after me, on to my head, knocking me out. When I came round, Tom made me promise to go to the doctor and confess all; the doctor said he would not report me if I promised not to fly again with test pilots.

It was now three months since the Battle of Alamein. At the end of November the British Army had started its rapid advance across the Libyan desert and since then conditions in Cairo had altered radically. No longer a fortified citadel, it was blossoming into the fleshiest of flesh-pots for the victorious army. By March I had saved up enough leave to withdraw some flesh from the pot and spend six days in Palestine. Peter was writing regularly; he would take a room for me at a suitable guest-house in Haifa. I went up with a girl from another watch, Audrey.

In Jerusalem we stayed at the King David Hotel and despite the snow, spent two days seeing all the sights, taking a bus out to Bethlehem. There were in those days few street vendors and fewer tourists so it was possible to see the monuments without being pestered, to walk along the Via Dolorosa, quietly stopping where one would. The little shops, the houses clinging to rocky hillsides, the bright-eyed children, the men and women in their long robes, were more evocative than the great monuments in bringing the reality of the New Testament to life.

From Jerusalem I took a bus to Haifa. It was a golden day, the sun in our eyes as we descended that tremendous road to the sea. The snow gave way to a blaze of early spring flowers. I had a window seat; many fellow passengers spoke German to me, all were very polite. That evening I would be with Peter. I wondered if it were possible to be happier.

The guest house was near the staff college. There were wonderful views but it was bitterly cold, a gale wind blowing in from the sea. Peter, tall and handsome in his uniform, arrived soon after I did. For the first time we could meet over several days. In other circumstances we might well have found that we had little in common. He was ten years older than I, more conservative, more traditional in every way. He spoke but little of his home in Leeds, of the grammar school he had attended, of how he had been accepted by the RAF and sent to London University to read economics.

He was not interested in books and ideas like my father, not laughing and dashing like Tom and the air crews with whom I fooled around, and was scornful of those who took every opportunity for sightseeing. Yet he had a way of looking down when he smiled; his eyes laughed when he was telling a joke. He was protective and considerate, had strong ideas of what a woman should and should not do, yet never forced these ideas down my throat. He was a hard worker and took pride in his job; even in wartime few men went to staff college while still in their twenties. He never even suggested coming up to my room. In the three days I spent in Haifa I fell seriously in love. Thoughts of him filled every moment of every day.

When Peter was working during the day I took trips, to Nazareth, to the Jordan. On our last night little Audrey had arrived to join me, and Peter came round to fetch us both. I was wearing the only mufti I possessed, an embroidered blouse and full skirt. Mufti was allowed on leave in Palestine, but Peter made me change back into uniform, cleaning my tunic buttons for me while I dressed. Then he took us out to the officers' club, where all his friends had gathered. I thought this was it, now we are engaged; never before or since have I been more flattered and praised, surrounded by all those staff college men putting themselves out to be pleasant to me. When Peter did not propose I felt sure it was because Audrey was there. He would when we met again, in two weeks' time. He would have to pass through Cairo to join his unit in the desert.

For wartime it was not a hard parting. Peter took us down to the station. He looked with horror on the conditions in which we would have to travel. Because we were women we had been put in the civilian part of the train. Cairenes were returning to Cairo now at a steady rate. There were ten women and children in a small carriage, its windows boarded against attack from the air. Realizing no food was available, Peter dashed off to buy us something, but could find only oranges. The train kept stopping, the children cried, there was no heating and no light, the oranges did not go far among twelve people. We arrived six hours late in Cairo and only reached TME just in time for me to go on duty.

A few days later I went on the morning watch feeling fuzzy, my throat throbbing. After half an hour I knew I must go up for air, but fainted before I reached the end of the long passage. As I had a temperature I was taken direct to the hospital in the Heliopolis Palace Hotel, about two miles away. I sat in the great hall with the stately double staircase rising out of it and with my imagination fired by fever I could see what a ball here must have looked like in times of peace. Certainly the room kept whirling round me as if I were waltzing, and there were flashes of colour before my eyes.

The hospital was full. Eventually a bed was found for me at Aboukir Hospital, now returned from evacuation, where the riding club was. Four hours had been spent waiting around so by now my temperature was a hundred and five and I felt extremely ill but the doctor – with every encouragement from me – insisted it was only tonsillitis and not diphtheria. Afterwards I decided it could well have been a reaction to the vaccine we had been given. I was determined to be discharged by the weekend when Peter came down. With any luck I would have some sick leave. The main problem was to reach him with messages.

His arrival was delayed, my return expedited, and by the time he rang up I was back on duty. I only saw him twice. After leave and sickness I could not ask for more time off, but how I longed for it. Sexual desire was stirring in me; I longed to sleep with him, and recalled my father's words. Peter didn't ask me. It never occurred to me to make the suggestion myself.

He had a horrid little room in the Continental Hotel, strewn with belongings as he sorted kit accumulated over two years into what he needed for the desert and what he would discard. We said goodbye on a moonlit night in April, outside the Anglican Cathedral where there is a little square overlooking the river. He held me in his arms and kissed me. We both knew we would be lucky to meet again. Peter was leaving at dawn, and I had to be on duty at 1.30 am. He insisted on sending me all the way back in a taxi.

I was glad to join A-Watch in the dining room and to join in the gossip, good to have my mind engaged by the niceties of the Enigma machine. It left no time for weeping and wailing. And I had a plan in the back of my mind: I still wanted to learn to fly.

# Chapter 7
## The Birthday Party

The Eighth Army's air umbrella was moving across the desert, reoccupying all the sites abandoned a year earlier. All the records of men, machines, and supplies to keep this enormous army moving passed through our hands in Cairo. The work was unremitting, but our numbers had been reinforced by new arrivals from England, so we were back on the four-watch system. This was as well, as the air-conditioning still had not arrived and the weather was settling into summer heat.

The war news on our front was so good, that summer of 1943, that it was decided to give a party to celebrate the WAAFs' twenty-first birthday. I think it should have been celebrated the previous year, when we were all so preoccupied with the possible evacuation of Cairo that celebrations had not seemed in order. Invitations were sent out to all the big-wigs, with Air Chief Marshall Sholto Douglas as the guest of honour. A dance floor was laid on the sand outside the mess, and the cooks went into overdrive, so busy creating wonders for the great day that our current meals were overlooked. On the day itself A-Watch came off duty at 1.30 p.m. I had a bunch of letters in the mailbox in the hall and stayed there to read them, while the others went in to lunch. The flight officer, Joy, came to find me.

"June, the new CO wants you – he's in the dining room!"

"Oh dear, what have I done this time?"

"It's not what you've done, rather what you're going to do. Haven't you heard?"

"Heard what?"

"You're the one who has to… Oh there you are, sir. This is Section Officer Watkins." She faded into the background. The CO was quite new, and we had not spoken before. His predecessor had been something of a rough diamond, coming into meals without his shirt and telling blue stories to shock the WAAFs. This wing commander was very different, an old Etonian, always correctly dressed and with a friendly manner designed to put junior officers at ease.

"Section Officer Watkins, I understand you are twenty-two!"

"Er… yes, sir!"

"But you were twenty-two when you volunteered two years ago." He must have been looking at my papers and had caught me out nicely.

"Yes, sir!"

"What do you mean, yes sir, no sir, butter wouldn't melt in my mouth, sir. I don't usually press ladies to tell me their ages, but I do need to know how old you are. I can assure you I would not dream of disciplining a lady over a little misunderstanding over her age!" He was laughing at me. I would be honest.

"I'm twenty this week, sir!" How old that sounded.

"It's your birthday? That's splendid. I suppose you know you are the vice-president of this mess?"

"Me, vice-president? I've never attended a meeting. I'm always on duty or sleeping!"

"Quite so. Watch-keeping officers are usually excused mess duties, but not when all the officers in the mess are watch-keepers. As the youngest officer and the most recently commissioned, you are the vice-president. Tonight you have to make the first speech, then when I have followed and the AOC has said his bit and the Queen Bee has said hers, you and I have to cut the cake."

"I… I can't make speeches, sir!" My face went scarlet at the very idea, remembering how tongue-tied I had been in Khartoum.

"Never yet known a woman who couldn't! You needn't speak for more than five minutes!"

I mumbled: "Yes, sir" and turned away. He put his hand on my shoulder and turned me round.

"You know, you must have been the youngest serving officer in the whole Middle East when you came up, man or woman, unless others were telling even larger fibs. That was quite an achievement in itself.

Can you really claim timidity? Why not use that quotation of Mussolini: 'Youth is a disease from which we all grow better every day'!"

Was it a coincidence, or was that damn quotation written in my papers? He felt in his tunic pockets and produced a folded sheet of signal paper.

"If you're really stuck, you could read this out. One of the pilot officers writes poetry of a kind and wrote it for the occasion. We'll meet here at 7 p.m. and wait for the AOC."

"Yes, sir." I was resigned. I would just have to make a speech. A-Watch was finishing lunch by the time I joined them, and we sat round the table discussing my fate. Topsy picked up the pilot officer's poem and read it out loud. It was sentimental doggerel of the variety found on greetings cards and was received with roars of laughter and unanimous condemnation – there were at least three English graduates on our watch, and two or three others who wrote. I repeated the quote the CO had suggested, and told them I had used it at my selection board.

"Then tell that story!" said Topsy.

"How?" I asked. She turned the poem over to write on the reverse side. Joy, our flight officer, moved over to help her. They had been at university together. In fifteen minutes they had covered the sheet and passed it to me. Mrs Garston, our actress, intercepted it, rose to her feet and read it out. It was perfect: gracious, short, witty, to the point. I tried reading it and after the third go they clapped and smiled at me. We trooped over to our quarters to sleep, for after the party we had to go on duty again.

It was stifling hot that afternoon, our little concrete boxes were like ovens, the temperature inside them over ninety-five. Outside, the glare on the sand was blinding. I lay naked on a towel which was soon damp with sweat and my skin itched all over. As I tried to doze off, the horror of the evening loomed over me, and I found myself repeating the words over and over again. A picture of my mother came to mind, walking round the farm in her muddy old slacks, a straw hat stuck on her head, a tangle of dogs round her feet, repeating as she went her maiden speech for the Legislative Council. I repeated mine to the blank walls, and then practised it with suitable gestures, finally using my hat as the cake I would have to cut.

Joy ordered a late tea tray from the mess; A-Watch congregated round me like a bunch of bridesmaids, brushing my hair, straightening my clothes, bemoaning with me when I laddered my last pair of silk stockings. Khaki silk stockings were hard to come by even in Cairo. Ten minutes early, I went over to the mess alone, and walked nervously up and down, waiting for the CO. He too was punctual.

"Are you as nervous as I am?" he asked.

"More, much more so, sir!"

"You know something? I don't see why you should have to make a speech if you don't want to. I'll say the thank yous for you, and you can cut the cake! I don't know why we didn't think of that before!"

The weight off my mind was terrific. I started to notice and enjoy the scene: the decorated food being carried out and arranged on huge trestle tables set on the sand; the band assembling and setting up their instruments; our own officers starting to drift over from quarters. Car-loads of visitors arrived and the CO kept introducing me as vice-president. Now the sun had gone down, the thermometer dropped to about eighty and the stars loomed large in the dark sky. A year ago we had been on the edge of defeat, and now the only thing which had defeated us was the installation of the air-conditioning

We waited and waited for the A.O.C. to arrive but he never came, some problem between him and his dentist. When the message finally reached us some time after nine, we all fell on the food, the band started playing, the party took off so well it was difficult to make any speech, and the cake-cutting ceremony was accompanied by cheers and jeers aplenty. When just after 1 a.m. the bus arrived to take A-Watch on duty, it seemed much too soon.

*

I had always wanted to learn to fly. The Egyptian flying club, closed down in the flap, had re-instituted itself in a corner of Almara Airport. Greatly daring, I enlisted for flying lessons at the club's flying school. There was one problem – I could hardly turn up in uniform, but for us mufti was forbidden. Then I had a brainwave. Sports clothes were allowed everywhere, and aroused no suspicion. In the cold weather I wore jodhpurs, the ones I had bought at school for six shillings, and in the hot weather my tennis outfit – I had rather a natty divided tennis skirt in a shiny material called sharkskin. There were a number of other young English people there in sports kit. Gradually I learned that they were all members of the armed services, and included one other woman, a nursing sister.

The flying club's lesson schedules were totally disorganized as each of us had to wait for one particular plane and one instructor to be free at the same moment, so we spent a great deal of time sitting around talking. This was a new group for me, very cosmopolitan, united only by a love of flying. Among them were some acquaintances like Nico Henderson, later to become British Ambassador to Washington and Paris. I had met him several times the previous year when I had accompanied my uncle to the British Embassy; where he was the most junior attaché. As the two most junior people present we were usually seated together. He was kind enough to ask me to dinner several times. Neither of us was drawn to the other; I did not like the way he criticized the RAF and kept wondering why he was not in uniform. He told me I would never stick university once the war was over, I would find the regulations for women too restricting.

Another character was an elderly British major who had taken his A licence and was working for the one which would allow him to take passengers. As soon as he arrived, he would march round the airport, drooling over all the planes on the ground and pointing out their good and bad points to anyone who would listen.

The Egyptian instructor, Abdul, asked me to lunch. He looked very astonished when I turned up in an officer's uniform. As a native Cairene, he showed me a Cairo different from the ones I had seen, teaching me to bargain in the *mousque*, calling on people who lived in the tombs of that extraordinary cemetery known as the City of the Dead, and taking me to a fortune-teller. He shocked his mother by taking me home to his family. He had a sister of my age who could hardly believe the freedom I was allowed. He kept saying that I was an object lesson for her, and would encourage her to go out into the world. His mother could hardly suppress her anger.

His mother may have disapproved, but not nearly so much as the RAF did when they discovered I was having flying lessons. I had severe strips torn off me for irresponsible behaviour. I could not see that I had done anything wrong, as so many other members of the forces were taking lessons at the same club. It was a great sadness that I had to stop my lessons when my next one would have taken me solo.

Shortly afterwards I was posted to Ismailia. It was considered a plum posting, but Peter – to whom I had not mentioned the flying lessons until they were forbidden – insisted I had been 'given the skids', as he called being posted as a punishment. The main punishment from my viewpoint was separation from A-Watch, but there were to be plenty of plums for me to enjoy: my first real responsibility, and my first real brush with authority.

# Chapter 8
## Ismailia

Ismailia is a small town on the shores of Lake Timsah, one of the salt lakes through which the Suez Canal passes. The RAF base there was a peacetime station designed to provide protection for the canal. Now operations had moved on, and with them many of the aircraft, yet it was still staffed to undertake work which was rapidly receding to the other side of the Mediterranean. Despite the capitulation of Italy to the Allies, the Mediterranean continued to be a major cockpit of war, and it was no doubt wise to keep sufficient forces there to protect the canal, which was still the Allies' only waterway into the Middle East.

The cypher office was a small room in a camouflaged stone building which also housed the signals unit. There were only three cypher officers, and as the office had to be staffed for twenty-four hours a day, we did long watches and then had generous time off. During the last year, machines had become ubiquitous and had replaced book cyphers almost entirely. They were so much quicker to use so that the work took less time, and at night the officer on duty could often kip down on a camp bed in the office. In mid-summer it was so hot that I took my bed outside, so that I could watch the sun rise over the flat brown landscape. We always had to be fully dressed so we could start work immediately, should an urgent signal arrive.

There was a signals section of some forty men, and for the first time I found myself involved in administrative work. We had to censor all the letters of our signals section, a process that always embarrassed me. There was I, a young girl, reading the letters which mature men were sending to their wives and girlfriends, and often having to do it in front of them. I developed a habit of skimming through, looking for forbidden place names, not reading the sense.

Yet the censoring did not seem to worry the men; on the contrary, time and time again while I was reading, a man would be hovering behind me. When I had finished he would say, "Tell me, miss, what would you do about that?"

"About what?"

"About what's in that letter you've just censored. I thought as a woman you might know how she feels…"

"I just skim through for place names!" I would reply. Then, seeing the pain in his eyes, I would add: "What about some char?" and while the man had something to do I would re-read the letter. Suspicion would stare out of the page – of the Americans, of an old flame, of almost anyone. And pathetic pleas: do not leave me, if you have some one else's child I don't mind but come back to me.

He and I would settle down to a cosy chat about the problems of separated families. My experience of sex life was nil; but I was an avid reader of the agony columns in women's papers and so was aware of the problems that beset lonely women. This was the other side of that same coin. It came as something of a shock to realize that the presence of WAAFs overseas caused much heart-burning back home; we were a whole squadron of 'other women'.

"Do you remember birthdays and anniversaries?" I would ask, and sometimes, very occasionally, I was brave enough to say: "Why not rewrite this page, and tell her how much you love her!"

The only real help I could offer was a sympathetic ear and the suggestion of prayer. Sunday evening services were increasingly attended by signals men. The padre, a lively man who had supplemented a small income with freelance journalism, chaffed me and asked when I was going to march the entire signals unit down. When he discovered the need for counselling I had uncovered, he started talks for the men. He had been an agony aunt for a woman's paper so he knew his stuff.

We WAAF officers had a separate mess, a three-bedroomed bungalow with the usual wire mosquito netting all round it, inevitably nicknamed 'the bird cage'. In addition to the three cypher officers, there was an administrative officer looking after a big unit of Palestinian airwomen and a scientific officer. We all got on very well but the cypher officer with whom I was supposed to share a room was fanatically tidy and I have always been the opposite. She was a beautiful blonde, very scornful of us lesser mortals who did not go hunting in the shires. Fortunately she and I were never either on or off-duty together, so we did not need to see much of each other except for handing over shifts at agreed hours of the day or night. We were both good workers so the office ran smoothly.

The scientific officer invited me to share her room, although watch-keepers were not meant to share with those on regular hours. Fortunately she was nearly as untidy as myself and we soon developed a system – anything left lying about was chucked on top of its owner's mosquito net. Sometimes the mosquito nets became so laden that they collapsed, but more often they just drooped onto our faces and forced us to empty them. We became firm friends, a friendship that has lasted a lifetime. Winifred was just down from Oxford, where she had read physics. Any problem I threw up, she would subject to the patient scrutiny of a trained mind. It was just the mental stimulus that I craved.

Like me, she was keen to learn to sail, and on several occasions we set off together in one of the pram dinghies kept at the sailing club on the shores of Lake Timsah. Neither of us were proficient sailors, and twice we managed to upset even a pram dinghy and had to clamber astride it, where we waited ignominiously to be rescued. But as the summer passed we improved and I had a great time sailing round the various ships which now crowded the lake.

Unlike Winifred, I was often able to go out early in the morning when the wind was at its best and the canal at its busiest. The canal had become the main channel of supplies to the Desert Armies. Ships queued in the lake for their turn through the narrow channels north and south – men of war, merchant ships, troop carriers, tankers, mine sweepers, passenger liners. It was fun to sail round them and be hailed by them, and often to be invited on board. Once I met the stewardess on a British India ship on which I had sailed as a child, another time a young cousin who unknown to me had joined the Navy. To show nationality and prove identity, we always took our service hats, our identity cards waterproof-wrapped inside them.

In July the landings in Sicily had taken place; and two months later combined American and British troops landed in Italy and Italy capitulated. About two weeks later, in late September, my cyphers told me the Italian fleet was to capitulate formally to the Allies in Lake Timsah. I could not share this news with any of my friends as it was top-secret, but I determined to watch the ceremony from the lake.

The British fleet had arrived in the early hours and was already drawn up when I set out in my dinghy, WAAF cap firmly clamped to my head. Captains of the various British men-of-war were being welcomed aboard the flagship. The Italian fleet was steaming in to the lake, ship after ship, each dressed with British sailors. They drew up in a long curve to the north. Once they were in place the admiral's barge set out to fetch the Italian admiral and two of his henchmen from the Italian flagship to sign the capitulation. They arrived, splendidly dressed with their helmets and swords, and were piped on board with great ceremony. Half an hour later they left without their swords.

It was a warm day and the signing took place on deck. By sailing out some few yards I was able to watch the whole scene from my dinghy. When it was over, the loudspeaker was brought to my side of the ship, and a voice bellowed down at me: "Ahoy there, miss – Admiral sends his compliments, wants to know what a WAAF is doing watching him and his flotilla!"

"I'm looking for my cousins!" I yelled back – and wondered whether my voice would carry. It did, and provoked another question:

"Admiral wants to know, what name, miss?"

"Baillie Grohman!" I replied. I had now managed to manoeuvre the dinghy right under the ship and could hear easily, but I could hardly believe the next message.

"Admiral says, will you come to lunch with him?"

"I'm hardly dressed for such an occasion!" I stood up in swimming costume and uniform cap

Another silence. Then: "Admiral says, never mind. He will lend you a shirt!"

Who could resist such an invitation? A rating ran down the companionway to take charge of the dinghy. A large white shirt was held out for me, so big it reached my knees and the sleeves flapped over my wrists. I felt like a little girl trying on Mummy's nightdress. We sat down, about twenty of us; I was the only woman present. We had an uproarious lunch – there had been plenty of wine on the Italian ships.

October was not such a good month. The senior cypher officer was posted, leaving only two of us. This was no hardship as the work was gradually decreasing, but when Heather went down with jaundice at the same time as did the RAF signals officer, I found myself running both sections. Only once during six weeks did I dare leave camp, and that once was a fiasco.

To make up for the fact that I could no longer go sailing, I took up rifle-shooting, and managed an hour off every afternoon on the range. This was near the CO's bungalow, and when he found out I was shooting, he always asked me to tea afterwards. He became too friendly. To me he was a dirty old man – he must have been about forty. Finally he insisted that I went swimming with him, although as the only cypher officer I should not have left the camp. He said I should wear mufti, which was forbidden. Foolishly I did so. We were only going to the beach. But we did not go to the public beach we usually patronised; he turned the car in the opposite direction to a secluded stretch of the canal, where he asked me to take my clothes off. I declined, refused to swim, demanded to be taken back. He offered me money. I insisted, this time successfully, on going home. I felt so menaced by this man that I gave up rifle-shooting. It took me too near his house.

Towards the end of November a new cypher officer arrived, and once I had introduced her to the office I went off for a day's sailing on my own. With a heady sense of freedom I took my dinghy to an army camp on the far side of the lake where I had been offered lunch. Autumnal winds were blowing and I made the crossing in record time. I dallied too long over lunch, overlooking the fact that in the afternoon the wind dropped. I was due back on duty at 6 p.m.; at four the pram dinghy was wallowing only fifty yards from the Eastern shore. I began wondering how I was going to return at all. A fishing boat with an outboard motor offered to tow me. I accepted thankfully, and threw them the sheet. They had a huge sail as well as the motor and we seemed to be making good speed when the men insisted I move into their boat to lighten the dinghy. Reluctantly I did so. By five o'clock we were in the middle of the lake, could see right down the southern arm of the canal and were approaching the De Lesseps Memorial. The club was only half a mile away. I could still be on duty in time.

There were three fishermen on board, and I noticed the two older men exchange glances with the younger one, hardly more than a boy. He stood up, clambered down the deck towards me, and grabbed me, a straightforward sexual attack. I was taken by surprise, but stood up and brought into use the eyeball pressure grip my father had taught me. The young man retired rubbing his eyes; the two old ones urged him on. He came at me again and I lunged against him. The boat rocked. We both went overboard. I swam under water as far as I could. When I came up the young man was hanging on to my boat looking sulky, the two oldies were laughing so much they were wiping their eyes.

There was a big army camp just behind the De Lesseps Memorial, about five hundred yards away. I would have to swim for it. The water was very salt, and by now cold. The men did not come after me. I crawled ashore, almost opposite an army sentry. I thought I was dripping water but was actually dripping blood; my heel had a deep cut where I had stepped on a knife when I was tussling with the young man. I heard the sentry phone his duty officer:

"Bleeding WAAF here, sir, half drowned, says she wants a lift back to the RAF camp." I arrived back in an army truck ignominiously wrapped in an army blanket, and had considerable difficulty in getting myself and my escorts past the RAF guardroom gate. Not only was I half an hour late going on duty, but I had committed a far worse offence in losing my cap and my pass.

On duty that night I once again decoded a telegram for myself. *"Inform Section Officer Watkins her father very ill. Operation has failed. Very little hope."* I had not heard about this second operation and wondered if he was still alive or whether they were breaking bad news to me gently. Tears did not come, merely anger: anger at myself for joining up and deserting the man who loved me so much. A new cypher officer was due the following day to make up our number to three, and the work was dwindling. This time I would have no guilt in asking for a posting to Nairobi, a proper posting, not a compassionate one. And I would stay at home as long as I was needed.

Alas, in wartime even good intentions can rarely be achieved.

# Chapter 9
## Delay in the Desert

My two colleagues were senior to me, but had asked me to remain in charge of the office until they knew the ropes. Now it took me two hours to check the inventories and hand over to the senior one. Then I threw my luggage into the back of an open truck and climbed up after it. I was supposed to await further movement orders but decided I would be able to find a lift down to Nairobi quicker than the movement office could. Winifred accompanied me to Cairo, to help me get my papers together. We sat in the back of an open truck, enjoying the cool wind as we sped past the great posters which said: *"If you write yourself off…"* followed some yards further on by: *"…Can Your Parents Replace You?"*

It was only when I arrived back in Cairo in November 1943 that I realized how much the fortunes of war had changed. The city was not only crowded with servicemen, and many more women, than before, it was not only a great heaving fleshpot for leave and convalescence; it was now also the crossroad of world war transport. Now that Italy had collapsed and was invaded by the Allies, the crossroads which had been in Khartoum had moved north. Senior officers no longer had to fly from Britain to Takoradi and then Khartoum to reach India and Burma, they now came by flying boats to Cairo via Gibraltar and North Africa, and then on to the southern hemisphere. Also, Cairo had become the in-place to visit, the nearest elderly but venturesome VIPs could get to the action. However, sea passage through the Mediterranean was still closed to British shipping, with many enemy subs hanging round the western end.

I wanted to report to RAFHQME, still in the old Hotel Metropole, but I had a problem, I had no cap and without one would not be able to salute all the gold lace – as we called those senior enough to wear gold on their caps. I had a word with the driver and he took us to the officers' shop. Here they had WAAF caps in plenty but only in small sizes. I have a large head and my hair was stiff with sand from the journey.

"Why not try a forage cap, miss, lots of the young ladies wear them?" said the storekeeper.

Winifred also liked them and we bought one each. Properly dressed, we saluted our way into HQ and I reported as instructed to the group officer. Everyone was wearing blue uniforms, we were still in khaki. Groupie was once again sympathetic and had heard my news before I had. In fact, she had been trying to phone me that morning, only to hear that I was already on my way. I was to be posted permanently to Nairobi because the unit there was being expanded, and an air passage had been arranged for me. Only nobody had let me know, down at Ismailia. Nor could I understand why the East African Command was expanding now the East African campaign was over. Hailie Selassie was back on the Abyssinian throne, and soon war would be leaving North Africa altogether.

"There is no need to make your own travel arrangements this time," Groupie commented drily. "You are leaving tomorrow morning on a special flight! And for tonight you are booked into the Hotel Continental, because it's from there that the transport leaves at 5 a.m. I presume you have enough money to finance yourself? Keep the receipts and you can put in a claim!"

"Thank you, Ma'am, Very good of you to make the arrangements."

I saluted and turned to leave. She called me back. "And Watkins, I don't like having to tell off girls who are already in trouble, but your CO said you were wearing mufti. Is that true?"

"Yes, Ma'am, he invited me to go swimming with him and said that it was all right to wear mufti just down to the beach, but instead of going to the beach where we often went for an hour or so on Sundays, he turned the car the other way, took me to a secluded spot on the canal and almost as soon as we arrived ordered me to take my clothes off. When I refused, he said I would be well rewarded if I complied with his wishes."

"And what did you do?"

"I turned and walked away, about half a mile back to the road, and tried to hitch a lift – not so easy in mufti, and then he came back to the car and drove me back to the station, in complete silence. He hasn't spoken to me since!"

"Ah, I see, he's one of those. It's better to refuse to go out. I must say I was surprised as you didn't strike me as being interested in clothes, or how you look. Just look at yourself now. Your face is all right but just look at the rest of you!"

I certainly lacked that band-box look. My uniform was creased, shoes dusty, the buttons of my khaki tunic – worn for the first time in three months – were pale green. My hair was stiff with dust from the long drive in an open truck. I did not say anything.

"I suppose you travelled in an open truck," she went on, finding my excuses for me, "and came straight here?" I nodded and she went on mildly: "In the interests of your fellow officers if not your own, try and look a bit smarter when you travel tomorrow! There will be VIPs on board!" She was a clever woman, leaving me feeling guilty for letting the side down yet showing that her sympathy was with me. Winifred and I sat in the tiny hotel room into which the management had crammed a second bed and spent the evening cleaning buttons, polishing shoes, and getting my uniforms pressed.

The plane leaving at dawn the following morning was a small one detailed to transport two senior civilians down to Nairobi. The journey would take only two days instead of the four needed by flying boats. The total complement was only nine: a crew of three, two VIPs from England (a knight and a peer of the realm), three airmen urgently needed for aircraft maintenance, and myself. I looked at the flight plan with interest. We were to follow the Nile down to Maralal, then cross Kenya, taking a straight line to Nairobi. I knew every place by its number on the meteorological map fixed permanently in my head.

We boarded the little plane. I do not know what the peer was about. The knight was a king's messenger and carried a thin leather bag stamped with the royal coat of arms permanently locked to his left wrist, while the peer carried a bulging briefcase. I sat with the sergeant, the two airmen immediately behind us. Lunch boxes were put in my charge. How easy life seemed, no pregnant South African WAAFs to look after, no abrasive South African major to contend with.

However, I was learning that life is never so simple. Shortly after taking off from Luxor, where we had refuelled and taken on more water, we developed mechanical trouble and had to come down in the desert. The pilot knew the area well and made an excellent landing on a disused landing strip. Our maintenance airmen diagnosed the problem, listed the spare parts, and the radio operator spent an hour contacting headquarters. Help would be sent immediately. It was only nine o'clock in the morning.

In early December the desert seemed pleasantly warm rather than burning hot. It was a very long morning, and at about midday the pilot led us to the frieze of palm trees which marked the river bank. There we turned south and soon came to a tiny hostelry created to serve river traffic. A passable meal was rustled up for us.

The rescue plane circled us and landed near ours. The lord, the knight and the WAAF were left to entertain each other and airmen of all ranks set off for the plane We expected to wait two or three hours; in fact, we stayed there for three days, closeted together like the characters in an Agatha Christie thriller, except murder was somehow avoided, though only narrowly. The rescue plane had brought the wrong spare parts.

The fact that Britain had a coalition government did not mean that the different political parties were in agreement. The lord belonged to the Labour Party to whom he owed his lordship, the knight was hereditary, a staunch Conservative. The little inn in which we found ourselves had only two guest rooms and the only point on which these two men could agree – they argued incessantly – was that I, the only woman, should have one of the rooms, while they shared the other one. This infuriated the pilot, who felt that a good room was his due as senior officer. I was quite willing to cede to him but the old men were adamant. If I did not take the second room, they would have one each. So the pilot shared the side veranda with the crew, the airmen had camp beds on the back veranda. At meals we started off at three tables, crew and myself, airmen, civilians. Soon we were mixing every which way. I sat at a different table every meal, but was frowned upon when I joined the airmen. When the hotel ran out of water we had to remain unwashed. The river was full of bilharzia.

It would have been difficult to imagine a more disparate group of people from the same country. The VIPs could hardly speak to each other politely; the king's messenger, his briefcase strapped to his wrist even in this little hotel, was extremely courtly, stately in his movements and manners. He would hold the door open for me, but before I could go through it an uncouth young airman would quite likely blunder along, or the lord claim the privileges of rank and age.

There was only just enough to eat. We had fish for breakfast, fish for lunch, and fish for supper, always fried in palm oil and served with tomato ketchup, until the ketchup ran out. Worse still, after the first day – nothing more to drink. Nerves frayed. We lived in a state of unfulfilled expectancy, hoping every hour to be rescued from our oasis. Both the older men played chess and I fetched my chessmen from the plane, but the king's messenger declined after I had been foolish enough to win the first game.

The days dragged by for me in some kind of nightmare, worrying fruitlessly whether my father was dead or alive, what was happening to Peter, how far had the fighting moved up Italy? Every time we heard a plane, we dashed out, hoping it was the rescue one with the spare parts. On the second day another rescue plane did arrive, this time with the right spares, but it took a long time to fit them and departure was delayed until dawn.

Gremlins were certainly with us all the way on that journey. On the fourth day we left at dawn and landed at Maralal, where we were to have a very late lunch and refuel. Maralal is situated on the Nile and was an Imperial Airways staging post. It is also exceedingly hot, even in December. Ready to take off again, in the heat of the afternoon we sat dripping in the plane, to be told that once again there was engine trouble. We must spend the night. There were enough little rondavels for each of us to have one to himself; there was enough to eat and drink and sufficient water to wash; but the heat was stifling, the mosquitoes beyond bearing, and all of us were on edge. Even the chess began to pall.

It was not until late the following morning that we finally took off. My sister Pella was on the runway of the civilian airport to meet me.

"I'm so glad you've arrived at last," she said. "Dad has smartened himself up every day to receive you, and has looked so sad when you didn't come!"

He was in the same ward in the same nursing home as the year before. He looked older and frailer than ever. His hair was a luminous white, soft and curly. There was a sad expression round his mouth, but his eyes filled with love when he saw me. I told him my adventures as I sat holding his hand, and then went up to HQ to report in.

In the cypher office sat Mouse. She had been on A-Watch with me when I first reached Cairo, and in Nairobi during my last visit.

"How marvellous to see you! And when am I on duty?"

"Yesterday," she laughed, "and old Kiwi is quite convinced that you have been gallivanting somewhere with a wonderful young man, probably one of hers, and has it in for you."

"Was there no signal about the prang?"

"Prang? You pranged?"

"I've been sitting in the desert playing chess with a knight for the last four days; and mighty boring it was!"

"Well, leave out the knight part, Kiwi will go green. She'd have eaten him for breakfast. How long were you in the desert? Look, you scram and I'll cover for you. Can you make tomorrow afternoon?"

"Yes, of course. Thank you!"

"Step carefully, Nairobi, the old b's got it in for you more than ever. And keep January 20th free, will you, for a wedding."

"A wedding? Oh, Mouse, how wonderful!" I hugged her again. Some girls had all the luck. She had two flying type husbands in as many years; all I could show was a bundle of non-committal letters from an equipment officer. Was I playing my cards right?

Pella had waited for me. The short rains had begun; she skidded cheerfully along the muddy farm road, losing control when the conversation got too interesting. My nose told me that the coffee-picking season was in full swing, there was that familiar musty smell of rotting coffee cherry. I sniffed at it appreciatively – it had always meant home. Sheba was fatter than ever but still managed to bounce up and down to welcome me. Ronny's baby, Richard, was crawling all over the place; my room had been taken over as a store for her wedding presents and I was to sleep on the floor of the big sitting room.

"What happened to my bed?" I asked. "Surely the wedding presents don't need that!"

"We needed all the beds, dear, for the Italian prisoners!" Mother had come up from the coffee factory. She had been too busy to meet me. I too was strained and upset.

"What!" I yelled. "How many Eyetie officers do you think have given up their beds to enemy prisoners!" I was furious. Then I saw Mother's tired and haggard face and could have bitten my tongue out. We had all been trained since early childhood to sleep on the floor when necessary.

That evening, firelight gleamed on the pewter plates. The rug was a mountain of muddy dogs. Ronny bent her head over fine sewing for Richard's wardrobe. You could tell from her taut face that Pat, her husband, was in constant danger. He was with Wingate in Burma behind the Japanese lines. Pella sat with her spaniels, Topsy & Turvy, on her knee. I had photos to hand around.

"Dad looks better than I dared hope," I ventured.

"Don't hope," Mother said. "There isn't any. There was another large lump in the tummy, nothing more could be taken away, it will only be a matter of weeks, perhaps of days. But the doctors don't want him told. He's to come home next week end. It's better to die at home." She looked round at her assembled daughters.

"Thank you, June, for coming home, you've always put your father first. Thank you, Pella, for coming down on your weekend off and meeting her. I'll need all your help over the next few weeks. Ronny and Richard are a lifeline for me, always here. We've just got to carry on as best we can."

Father was dying in the middle of the coffee-pulping season, and there was to be an election to the Legislative Council early next year. We all knew that nothing would persuade Mother to give up either interest. None of us could imagine life without Father. I turned my thoughts to Peter.

Next day I reported for duty. The WAAF mess had moved from the primary school across the main road to the grounds of Government House, a brand new complex of huts. The cubicles were a little bigger than the last ones, the mess room much larger and more welcoming. Kiwi held her fire until supper.

"And where have you been gallivanting around?" she asked. "We heard you left on the twenty-eighth!"

"I did," I replied, "and we were held up just south of Aswan, we pranged."

"Do you really expect me to believe it took you six days to do a two-day journey?"

"Do you think I would have delayed in the circumstances? With my father dying?"

"That's what you said last time!"

"My mother's been told he can't last until Christmas!" I heard a note of aggression in my voice. How could I be haggling over my father's death like this? Kiwi smoothed her skirt and pursed her lips. It was a gesture that drove me mad.

"This time, June, I do think you should spend more time in the mess, and not cut all the social engagements. As the newest officer I want you to take over the bar, and as a local I think you should do the garden. Christmas is coming up, and we all want to have a jolly time together, so you will be here for the parties, won't you?"

"I'll do the garden gladly but I'd rather not do the bar. I don't know about drinks, and it's not going to be my year for a jolly Christmas."

"That's a very selfish way to talk, June, I'm sure things are not as bad as that."

Mouse caught my eye. Keeping silent can be an enormous effort. For once I made that effort. It is not always the best tactic. Worse was to come.

# Chapter 10
## Calamity at Christmas

Father was soon installed at home and insisted on working on a bumper edition of his paper, Baraza, for Christmas. When I had a few hours off I would pick up Francis, the African assistant editor, and drive him out to the farm to work with Father. The wireless was tuned in for every news bulletin – the fighting was particularly bitter in Italy that autumn

Kiwi refused to allow me to take any of the leave due to me, saying that as the most recently arrived officer it would be unfair to give me extra time off. We were much busier than before, the Allies were stocking up supplies to fight in Burma, Japanese submarines were busy in the Indian Ocean. The southern seas had to be swept from Durban to Mombasa, from Mombasa to Ceylon. I was happy to do my share of Christmas watches in the office; in the mess it remained difficult to avoid trouble.

First there was the cocktail party. I had been ordered to attend as I was, despite myself, the bar officer. It was the first Christmas we had spent in the new mess, and Kiwi was determined to make a splash. Everyone who was anyone had been invited: commanding officers of all the other camps, many important figures in civvy street, the bishop, even the Governor, Sir Henry Moore – he, wise man, had declined but was sending his sixteen-year-old daughter Jo instead. Jo and I had once been at school together, and I had been a friend of her elder sister. I liked Jo and looked forward to seeing her again.

The long, low mess hut looked attractive and welcoming; there were huge vases of flowers everywhere; a blazing log fire at one end of the room, and beside it the bar with an African mess steward and myself in attendance. We were most of us good-looking girls in our early twenties, now all dressed up in our war-paint and our best blue uniforms.

Mouse stood beside me, our heels on the stone kerb of the fire-place, and watched Kiwi receiving the first guests across the room. We were playing a popular game – commenting on every unknown man as he came in as to whether he would, or would not, ask us out. The rules of this game allowed you to comment only on men you had not met socially before. Meeting them on duty did not count. As a new girl, I could comment on most of the officers, while Mouse did not know the civilians. The rangy, good-looking group captain, who often stood in for the CO and liked to call in at the cypher office at midnight, came in.

"Yes," I said to Mouse.

"Nairobi, you must be joking! That's Kiwi's!"

"He can't be; he looks much too good for her."

"She's pursuing the poor man like a bitch on heat."

He strolled over to me. "You're the new girl I saw in the office the other day, aren't you? My name is Douglas-Hamilton."

"Yes and no, sir, I've only been back here a week or so, but I come from Kenya!"

"Oh, so you must be Olga Watkins' daughter. I met your mother a week or two ago. A very remarkable woman. You're having a difficult time, I gather…" Kiwi had caught up with him and had a hand on his shoulder.

"We'll have our conversation later," he said as he was led away. "What about dinner on Thursday?"

"I'm afraid I'm on duty, sir!" I lied.

Mouse looked at me. "You certainly won that round, Nairobi, but I wouldn't be in your shoes for all the world".

Jo Moore also arrived early; she was still at school, gauche, over-weight, jolly, and dressed like a rag bag. Jo's mother had accompanied her elder daughter, Deirdre, to South Africa and Jo was living wild while her mother was away. She never cared about clothes, comfort, or indeed any of the niceties of life. Now she ignored Kiwi, who was greet-ing someone else, walked across the room and fell on my neck. Soon we were arranging to ride together in the early mornings.

Then Kiwi was behind me. "I do think you might introduce important guests, and not keep them to yourself!" Kiwi tried to talk to Jo but Jo was at an awkward age and had little small talk – she liked books, horses and chess and wanted, like me, to go to Oxford University. Kiwi would have considered all four topics stuck up. Jo did not want to be an important guest, she did not want to be the governor's daughter, she wanted to be Jo. I found her simplicity endearing, Kiwi did not. When I had to busy myself at the bar, Jo stood gawping for a few minutes and then slipped out home.

The bishop arrived late; he came straight over to me to ask after Father and, sensing my unease, asked me why I was at a Christmas party when I would obviously rather be at home.

"There was not too much choice over the matter!" I said. Kiwi was behind me, looking daggers, pushing to be introduced.

A few evenings later it was raining hard. I had been home for my day off and brought back a load of plants for the garden. I put on my farm slacks and started planting in the rain. Sheba insisted on helping me, digging excitedly wherever I dug, and soon we were both covered in mud. Jo, wearing a sou'wester back to front and an old sack borrowed from the prisoners who worked in government house grounds, called in to arrange our riding for the next day. She carried another sack filled with muddy plants and started to work with me. Now and then we would sit back and discuss which plants should go where.

Kiwi was going out to some official party, escorted by the group captain. She stood on the top step above us, her face stiff with makeup, shoes and buttons shining, eyes glittering furiously.

"And what do you think you're doing?" she asked.

"Planting up the garden – the rain is just what we needed!"

"Indeed, I'll speak to you later. And who is your little friend?"

"Oh Ma'am, I introduced you the other night. This is our neighbour, Jo Moore. She's brought some wizard plants from Government House gardens. Isn't that kind!"

I saw her face tighten as she looked Jo up and down. Jo was covered in mud, it streaked her face, coated her arms up to the elbows and clung to the long bare legs sticking out from under the tattered sack. Kiwi was too angry even to greet or thank her, and moved on down the wooden steps in ominous silence. The group captain followed her dutifully, and caught my eye as he passed. We both managed to keep straight faces. Jo did not; she was laughing so much she fell on her face in the mud and I had to take her in for a bath before returning her to Government House.

For me, invitations to Government House proliferated. They were usually unofficial, often only to Jo's rooms, but she liked to ask me when her father had planned to dine alone with her, no doubt to talk to her about her behaviour, her refusal to comply with the norms of Government House.

"He can't tell me off when you're there, so do come!" Now and then he asked me himself; single girls who could be asked at the last minute were in short supply. Kiwi resented me being invited when she was overlooked. However hard I tried to slip out by a back gate used by sentries, she always seemed to see me, her eyes following me with hate and her lips with bitter remarks.

My father's birthday was on 23rd December. I did not forget it that year. I was not supposed to go home between watches but had decided to do so without telling Kiwi. As I had no car, I caught the early bus and walked three miles through the forest. I loved that forest walk, but this time it gave me no pleasure. My heel had never healed from the gash I had received when attacked on Lake Timsah three weeks before. It was growing more angry and swollen every day. Now it became so painful that I had difficulty in completing the last mile.

Father seemed better than usual, and wanted to drive me back to work. We compromised; I borrowed his car to go to work in the afternoon and returned for a late supper. For once it was only the family at home and we all sat round the fire. He read poetry to us as he often did, and when I had to go back to work for night duty, I kissed him goodbye cheerfully, promising to bring Francis out the next day with the proofs of the Christmas edition of the paper before it went to press.

There was little work that night but my foot was so painful, with such a throbbing in the groin, that it kept me awake when I might have slept. In the morning I limped over to the surgery. While waiting my turn I rang home to say I would be later with Francis than I had anticipated. Ronny answered.

"Don't bring Francis!" I could hear the strain in her voice. "Soon after you left last night, Dad collapsed, groaning with pain. The doctor said this is what he was expecting; he's arranged a nurse. His cough has turned into pleurisy. He'll be sedated all the time from now on."

It was my turn to face the RAF doctor.

"Straight into hospital with you," he said.

"I can't." And I told him what was happening at home.

"Is there a nurse looking after your father?"

"Yes."

"Right. As long as she understands she has two patients, not one. You must keep that leg up, all the time. No Christmas food, no drinks. The sulpha drugs don't go with either." Before the introduction of penicillin, sulpha drugs were used for all kinds of blood poisoning, and very depressing they were.

"There won't be any," I snivelled, "only coffee!"

"Coffee?"

"Yes, coffee drying everywhere. We live on a coffee farm." I was trying to be light-hearted.

"That sounds interesting," he replied. "I'll call in to see you, let me see – on the twenty-seventh."

"What about my work?" I asked.

"It'll be some time before you're back on duty! At least three weeks, probably more. I'm serious – in any other circumstances I would insist on hospital; I feel I should do so even now. It won't help your mother to have two disasters on her hands."

Was I really so ill? I certainly felt it, far too ill to tell Kiwi how long I would be away. "Will you tell… my flight officer for me?"

He patted my leg where it rested before him; it sent shoots of pain right through me.

"With the greatest of pleasure, my dear." Then he looked at me enquiringly. "Is that woman making matters worse for you?" I only learned later that he had crossed swords with Kiwi on several previous occasions. His kindness proved too much for me. I burst into tears. The doctor saw his last patients, and then put me in his car and drove me out to the farm himself, making sure the nurse knew I was ill. Then he drove all the way back again to bring in Pella to drive father's car home.

The nurse came in the daytime. My mother sat up at night. She would not let me take the whole nights from her, but agreed we should halve them. A footstool had been added to the easy chair beside the bed, so I felt medical instructions were being obeyed. On the night of the twenty-sixth I took the first part of the night, promising to call Mother at 2 a.m. But when the time came I could not bring myself to do so. Father was sleeping peacefully and Mother needed rest more than I did. Towards three his pain killers started to wear off, and he had a bad coughing bout. Coughing made the pain much worse. I tried to give him sips of water from his feeding cup. Mother put her hand on my shoulder.

"High time you went for some sleep –I'll do the rest of the night." At dawn she came in and told me it was all over, and went down to the garden near the big tree, her favourite spot on the farm, and decided just where to put the grave.

I was still in bed at eight o'clock, wondering when the doctor would arrive. I hugged Sheba and she licked me. I could not face the new day, the first day without Father. Ronny and Richard arrived from the next room.

"Do get up, June, there's so much to do."

"I'm expecting my doctor," I said grandly, thinking how pleased he would be with me. For the first time in weeks the foot was not throbbing. The sulpha drugs and rest had worked. "Anyway, what can I do?"

"Well, you could do the phoning. Ma's already phoned the radio station and they put the announcement on the early news. The funeral will be at half past two. She's out now digging the grave with all the Italian prisoners." In the Tropics, before the days of deep freeze, funerals had to take place within twenty-four hours. If Mother could face the world, so could I. I put on one of my old farm smocks and hopped across to the telephone.

"Breakfast?" Ronny called out.

"No thanks, couldn't. Some coffee, if it's drinkable."

"No worse than usual. Come and look at this, it'll cheer you up."

Richard was fifteen months old. He sat in his high chair, golden hair brushed up in a quiff above his high forehead, his large blue eyes fixed solemnly on his plate, a spoon grasped in each chubby hand as he tried to feed himself. Food was plastered all over his face and was shooting in all directions – an Alsatian lay on either side, cleaning up the pieces as they dropped. He was a beautiful child, and so like his grandfather. I had never wanted a child before. Now I did, lots of them, just like Richard.

I turned to the telephone and made the first call. It was to our neighbours, the Graham-Bells, market gardeners and coffee farmers who had been so good to my parents years ago. My father had met Harry forty years earlier in the Boer War. Harry had already heard, on the early radio news. "We're coming over to do the grave. Just about to leave, the van's loaded. Don't let your mother worry about anything – the grave, the flowers – I'm coming with my team to do the lot."

I was still at the phone when his market van arrived, laden with flowers, tools, labourers. Harry drove down the grassy walks, and drove back again with Mother. Ronny fetched her coffee, made her sit down, anchoring her by placing Richard firmly on her knee. Harry and his team finished and neatened the digging, lined the entire grave with flowers, heaping more all over the raw red earth until nothing was to be seen but mounds of blue and white lilies, carnations, roses, never have there been such flowers as those. The Graham-Bells' estate was Nairobi's leading market garden, and with the onset of the rains it was in peak condition.

Our garden also looked magnificent. Father had laid it out twenty years before, the year I was born, as a series of grass walks with wide herbaceous borders leading through the dark green coffee bushes to copses of huge trees surviving from the virgin forest which had once covered the land. Everything was flowering after the rains: pale blue potato creeper and fiery golden shower over the house, crimson bougainvillea over the cart sheds, lilac jacarandas all round the lawns, creamy white frangipani and moon-flowers at intervals along the borders to mark divisions of colour, in one section only red flowers and shrubs, in the next yellow, then orange, blue, and white. At the end, as we approached the grave, was Father's favourite and latest bed, a smelly garden, where only sweet smelling plants were allowed. Frangipani and moon flowers stood stalwart among a profusion of scented geraniums and roses.

The funeral was at 2.30 p.m. We were amazed at the number of people arriving. Funerals had to be held at such short notice, this one was in the middle of a long holiday weekend, and petrol was strictly rationed. Yet the cars kept rolling up. We had expected about fifty people, not five hundred.

We processed down the grass walks to the grave. I was limping behind the coffin carrying my father's medals on a cushion. As we reached the grave, the cortege had to turn left and I could see the crowd following us, nearly all the men in khaki, the government officials smart in khaki suits, the farmers in much laundered khaki drill, the younger generation in khaki uniforms. Most of the women were in their only tidy suit – a suit was considered much smarter than a cotton frock – and that too was usually made of khaki cloth, it was a practical colour for dusty Kenya roads. The Africans wore their brightly coloured Sunday best. There was not a black outfit to be seen anywhere. Among the crowd, conspicuous in their blue uniforms, were the group captain, Kiwi, and two of my colleagues.

We sang: "The day thou gavest Lord is ended" and the Nunc Dimittis: "Now lettest thou thy servant depart in peace…" Even today, either of those psalms transports me straight back to that grave, to the serious faces and the best clothes of wartime Kenya. Around me everyone wept. For me tears did not come.

Funerals in Kenya were usually short affairs – one could not offer refreshments to so many at such short notice. It was customary to offer condolence only when departing. We four women stood in a row shaking hands, saying, "Thank you for coming." The group captain led his group over to me and said a few suitable words. Kiwi never missed an opportunity.

"When are you coming back to work?"

"You'll have to ask the doc that, Ma'am. I don't know. He was supposed to visit me today and he didn't come!" I looked down at my feet, the right one covered with one of Father's socks over the bandages.

"Well, you're walking about and obviously quite recovered, and we're having to do your work."

"I'm sorry about that!" I said.

The group captain had put a firm hand on her shoulder, turned her round and led her away. She turned her head for a parting shot: "So are we!"

Mouse hugged me: "Don't forget – January 20th, my wedding day!"

"I'll be there, doctor's orders or no doctor's orders!" I said, doing my best to look happy.

As the crowds dispersed we retreated into the house. "Well, that's the end of one era and the start of a new one!" Ronny spoke through her tears. None of us knew how short the new era would be.

# Chapter II
## The Wrong Direction

It was mid-January before I returned to work. The effects of the blood poisoning had worn off and so had the effects of the sulpha drugs. I was regaining that wonderful feeling of youth, that I could do anything, even get on with Kiwi. I would run the bar cheerfully and do what I could to placate her. It was not easy.

On the day I arrived back, I sat in the mess waiting for lunch. Kiwi came in. "So there you are at last! Did you have a good long holiday? Did you enjoy dancing at Torr's Hotel on New Year's Eve?"

"I haven't been dancing since I arrived here!" I said

"Are you accusing me of lying? I saw you there myself. The group captain stopped to speak to you. You were wearing mufti." She was growing dangerously angry.

I calmed my voice. "Not of lying, Ma'am, only of mistaken identity. My sister was there but I wasn't. She's often mistaken for me. Clearly the group captain was also mistaken!"

"Very clever! Very clever indeed, but you won't get away with it."

At that moment Mouse came in. She looked flushed and prettier than ever and was laden with shopping. Her fiancé, equally laden, followed her in.

"Welcome back in good time for the wedding! A funny thing happened just now, we saw your double in the car park, she was in mufti, of course, but when I saw her climb into the sort of car you drive, I called out and she waved at us and called back, 'I'm not June, I'm Pella!'"

"Mother says she can't understand it – she's five years older than me and much prettier!" I laughed and Kiwi stalked out of the room, fury written on her face.

"What's bitten her?" Mouse asked. And when I told her, she warned me to be more careful than ever.

Kiwi had limited my time off so I could only return home for the night one day a week, usually at short notice. Meanwhile Lady Moore had returned to Government House, and she told me she was delighted that Jo had at last brought home a sensible friend, and hoped that I would come round as often as I could as it was lonely for the girl now that her sister was at university. She hoped I would try to persuade her daughter to dress more suitably and to attend some of the formal dinners. Jo had announced that she would only attend the dinners if I was invited, because she wanted someone less boring than the Governor's ADC to talk to! This suited me fine. I particularly enjoyed riding up through the arboretum and on the other side of the Nairobi River to the Delamere Estate. There were stretches of undeveloped land across which our ponies would amble while we had a good natter and giggle; sometimes Jo's pony would turn his head and look at her as if to say: "What on earth are you up to now?" Then, as soon as we turned, they were all restlessness and wanting us to race them back to their stables.

I also much enjoyed a number of good dinners when extra women were needed, and apparently I looked smart enough in my best blues to please Lady M's exacting standards. It was a wonderful escape hole for me and so near that it even counted as being on call when I was duty officer. The sentries from GH came through to our mess by a special gate to do our flag raising and downing for us, and as I also used the gate, I often met the sentries and watchmen. As I was the only officer who could speak Swahili, they chatted to me. Kiwi told me not to be so familiar with them, a command I happily ignored.

She was even more annoyed when the group captain sent for me and told me that the RAF were again running a recruiting drive for more WAAFs. This time they wanted other rankers rather than direct entry officers, and were happy to take girls down to the age of twenty-one. Now that the fighting had moved to Italy, living conditions in the Middle East were much easier and they needed women to replace tour-expired men in office jobs in Egypt. They wanted me to do some broadcasts encouraging local girls to join up. I got Jo to help me write the broadcasts as she knew what would appeal even better than I did and had a wonderfully quick turn of phrase. Broadcasting was live in those days and I had to make several trips up to the Kenya Wireless station at Kabete. My dog Sheba accompanied me everywhere and for some reason during the first broadcast she gave a loud yap just when I said it was hard leaving home. Everyone congratulated me on training her to do it, but she had just done it of her own accord.

The broadcasts had the desired effect and brought in dozens of enquiries The same admin squadron leader who had recruited me just two years earlier came down from Cairo to make her selection. She sent for me and used my local knowledge of the families. As always, the first consideration was security.

Suddenly she changed tack. "Do you still want to go to Italy?"

"Yes, very much!" I replied, knowing Peter would be crossing any day.

"Then you are thinking your posting to the Seychelles is a step in the wrong direction?"

"The Seychelles? Me? When?"

"You mean your flight officer hasn't told you? We have to relieve the girls there in about June!"

I was already late for my watch, so I said goodbye and saluted. As I turned to go she called out, "Come back! Sit down! Take your cap off! That's better!" She was using a kinder voice than the brusque tone she had used before. "May I give you some advice? This is not official, it's an older woman speaking to a younger one. If you want to avoid trouble in the services, or in civvy street for that matter, don't go off with other people's boyfriends, particularly not those of your senior officers."

Ah, that was why I was on my way, and I did not even fancy the group captain, he was far too old!

"I've hardly been out, let alone got off with anyone's boyfriend since Father died." I was genuinely puzzled by the accusation.

"But you have been out with the group captain?"

"Certainly not," I said, "I haven't been going out with anyone except a schoolgirl, and some old friends from the Met office." And then I remembered. "Group Captain Lord Nigel calls in at the Cypher Office most evenings at midnight. He looks through the 'Most Immediate and 'Top-Secret' baskets. He always asks me lots of questions about Kenya, about the people and the country .and where to visit – that kind of thing.

"One day, during our recent elections, he asked me if I knew the Chief Native Commissioner, one John Willie Hoskins. When I said that I not only knew him but he was in fact my guardian, Lord Nigel asked if I could arrange a meeting. He was not a member of a club so would I suggest a suitable venue for a meal, somewhere where we could talk? I suggested the Lobster Pot, and then he asked me to bring my mother along as well as he wanted to talk to her too. My mother was amused because I had to act as hostess and she said that I had done well to put Mrs Hoskins near myself where I could listen to her talking about her children whom she hadn't seen for five years. Mother knew that I would much rather have talked Kenyan politics with herself, John Willie, and Lord Nigel. He brought me back to the mess afterwards. That has been my one and only social contact with the lord!"

*

It was now nine months since I had left TME, where we did the signals for Combined Allied Headquarters in the Middle East and were aware of the long-term planning of the war. Military action had passed from Kenya nearly three years earlier, so I had been surprised when I heard that RAF East Africa was expanding. What was happening? The reason soon became clear. Since the fall of Singapore in 1942, sea passage across the Indian Ocean had been threatened by Japanese submarines. A full-scale attack on Japan would need a stockpile of military equipment, but convoys carrying the supplies were being attacked all the time. RAF East Africa had now to concentrate on their destruction, and on the prevention of the Japanese Army occupying any of the Islands as bases. Operational stations had been set up around the Indian Ocean, flying sea-planes called Catalinas. The main problem was that a sea-plane needs calm water to land safely; a swell of less than eighteen inches is recommended. The Indian Ocean is rarely calm, in many places there is a constant swell of around three feet, in the monsoons considerably more. Lagoons and harbours had to be carefully selected.

I imagined the Islands would be like our family Shangri-la, where we had spent wartime holidays in a tiny coastal cottage at Nyali Beach, north of Mombasa, long before that beautiful place had been destroyed by great tourist hotels. I saw myself languishing in the heat, swimming every day from a golden coral beach shaded by palm trees, doing a little bit of work of an evening. Ignorance can be bliss. Now I was to learn from experience what life on such an island could be like.

# Chapter 12
## The Seychelles

On my twenty-first birthday I woke up in the RAF mess of 205 Squadron at Port Reitz, just south of Mombasa Island. It was before dawn, the sun no more than a pink promise over the sea. My colleague Doreen and I packed and dressed quickly. It was my turn for the secret bag; it weighed about five pounds and Doreen locked it to my left arm. Carrying my suitcase in my right hand, I went downstairs in search of breakfast. It was an operational squadron and breakfasts had to be good and punctual.

WAAF were not meant to fly on operational flights, but the only way to reach the Seychelle Islands, other than by a long sea trip, was to fly in an RAF Catalina. There was a regular mail flight from Mombasa to the Seychelles, but even this was expected to carry out an anti-submarine sweep when necessary. So the first, and last, operational flight of my career was on my twenty-first birthday, in a Catalina flying from Mombasa to the Seychelles.

We left the RAF mess at dawn, there were six members of crew and two other passengers for our flight. The launch was waiting, the lagoon mirror-smooth, and once on board, the crew disappeared to their various cubbyholes and we passengers – there were two others as well as ourselves – sat in the dimly lit cabin on the lower bunks, facing each other, unable to see out or even to read. There was a tiny galley, just large enough for us to cook ten omelettes for lunch – we also opened two bottles of lukewarm champagne someone had smuggled into the plane for my birthday. We reckoned a fifth of a bottle each would not upset the crew. It took us time to cook the omelettes but as the crew had to hand over one to another before each man could eat, and the table would not take more than four, this suited us all fine.

We flew at something over a hundred miles an hour, so the one thousand-mile flight took around ten hours, depending on the wind and what detours were considered necessary. We travelled mostly in silence. It demanded extraordinary concentration from the pilots, flying only fifty feet from the waves hour after hour – a second's lapse of attention would have landed us in the drink. Equally, the navigator had a difficult job. The Islands are tiny pin-pricks in the ocean; a fraction of a degree out and we would have missed them altogether. Cats did not carry sufficient fuel to reach the next port.

There were no windows in the galley but the midship gunner had a splendid view. The latrine bucket was in his cabin, and to use it we girls had to move him to guard one door, while the rear gunner had to be asked to stay put while we were in occupation. We girls found this very embarrassing, yet we longed to linger in the makeshift loo because the view was so good. I spent the last part of the journey sitting on the floor of this compartment, looking out over the Indian Ocean for the Islands to appear.

At last the tiny group of islands showed up green and white against the grey-blue which characterizes the Indian Ocean. I have always wondered that each of the world's great oceans has its own particular shade of blue. We circled Mahe, the largest island, saw the launch put out, and came down in the harbour. Even here it was like a switch back. We went on heaving up and down after the plane came to a standstill and was tethered to the buoy. I just managed to keep the omelette and champagne down until we were in the launch.

The RAF station was a small seaside hotel, complete with miniature swimming pool. An open-sided annex through which the monsoons howled had been added to provide a dining room and bar. The cypher office was in an upstairs room opening onto a balcony overlooking the bay. That first evening I stood groggily on the balcony watching the twilight turn into night. Immediately beneath me, high tide brought waves splashing up through holes in the coral. Two Catalinas were bobbing about on their buoys; the Imperial Airways flying boat, Golden Fleece, her recently holed bottom stuffed with cement, was wallowing heavily to quite a different rhythm. A great darkness descended on me, an acute awareness that some tragedy was going to occur.

"Ah, there you are, June, welcome!"

Rob Graham-Bell came out of the darkened room behind me. He was the son of our neighbours, a close friend of my family, a short brawny man with bright red hair, noted both for his courage and his short temper. The temper was attributed to the fact that he was often in considerable pain from his club foot, a disability to which he made no concession and no one dared mention. Far greater than any physical pain was the hurt that he – a keen peacetime pilot – had not been accepted for operational flying. In a weak moment he had confessed to me: "Bader, with no legs, is allowed to fly, but I'm not. A woman could do the job I'm doing!"

"I'm so glad that you're not flying, Rob, you're such a good neighbour and we all know what happens to wartime pilots," I said politely but I was thinking: "I bet women would make damn good pilots if they were only given the chance!"

Rob had already accomplished much in his life, both as a pioneer pilot and motorist, driving cars where they had never been driven before. He had pioneered the route across the Sahara, and across Africa in many other directions. He drove an old Rolls Royce, and had proved a kind neighbour, braving extra miles of our excruciating farm track in order to give me a lift to RAFHQ while my father was ill. Now he was my CO, I wondered how we would get on. His father was notorious for his old-fashioned ideas about women. Had Rob, I wondered, inherited those ideas?

There were only five officers on the permanent staff. Rob was officer commanding, there was an army engineer attached to us who looked after our signals, a meteorological officer, and us two WAAFs. Our predecessors had to leave the next day on the same Catalina that had brought us in, and all evening we found ourselves signing paper after paper concerning our new responsibilities. It was after eight before the other two went off to pack.

Rob escorted Doreen and me into supper in the long thatched annex. Over the meal he explained how the station worked. There were not many cyphers, probably not more than forty or so a day. In the old days of book-cyphers this would have kept two full time cypher officers busy; now that outstations had machines it meant a mere four hours' or so work. Cypher officers were traditionally exempt from administrative duties; in the present circumstances they could not be. Doreen was senior and had to be responsible for the cypher office and all equipment. She was also responsible for manning the radio equipment to bring planes in. As I had already discovered in our signing session, I was to be imprest holder, pay officer, and caterer.

If Operation Overlord (the D-Day landings in Normandy, which had taken place earlier that month) continued as successfully as it had started, the war in Europe was expected to be over in months. The battle of the Indian Ocean, which had to be won before we could think of invading Burma, let alone Japan, was only just starting. There were half a dozen squadrons each of six aircraft stationed on bases round about; Diego Suarez in Madagascar, Mauritius, Adu Atoll, Kogalla, Mombasa, Dar-es-Salaam. The effectiveness of these squadrons was greatly strengthened by a policy of concentration. When a convoy was coming through, all the squadrons congregated in one base and systematically swept the seas before them. They stayed only a few nights, and then moved on, ahead of the convoy. Each of the stations would host the Catalinas when necessary, and in addition several other bases such as the Seychelles and the Maldive Islands, where the swell was too high for regular use, had been set up for occasional use. The occasions were becoming more frequent.

Each Catalina carried an operational crew of six and a maintenance crew of ten. The entire crew flew to whichever base was selected, dumped the maintenance crew and went off on operations. As each Catalina returned, the maintenance men went to work, all night if necessary, to have the planes ready for the next sortie.

This made the flaps (as periods of increased activity were called) more demanding. RAFHQ in Seychelles had only a skeletal organization to handle them. During a flap, the number and importance of cyphers increased tremendously. At the same time there might be twenty or more Catalinas to talk down in the evening. Our call sign was "Glamour", in honour of the fact that this was the only station with WAAFs. All this was to be Doreen's responsibility, although I too would have to take my turn. Quiet periods between flaps had to be used to get everything organized for the next one.

As imprest holder, I had to sign for all domestic equipment issued to the station and check that it was maintained in reasonable condition. My main problems would be providing food and pay for numbers that might vary in a few hours from our normal strength of just over forty to four hundred or more. The hotel had adequate gardens, grass huts and tents were easy to erect; there was plenty of rain water, the climate was warm. The only problem was food. I had to be ready for increasing numbers at any time. My predecessor had found the Army catering officer intractable and had quarrelled with him. Rob hoped I would use charm instead of argument.

When Rob had finished we sat on over our coffee. It was disgusting. Both his parents and mine had tons of coffee they could no longer export piling up on the other side of the Indian Ocean.

"Couldn't we arrange for some decent coffee, Rob? Your parents and mine would both donate it," I suggested.

"Now I told you, June, don't start trying to improve the food – you'll only antagonise that brown job and make matters worse!". Despite the put-down, I was impressed with Rob.

"How many young men landed in a forsaken outpost could give such a clear exposition of the war and their part in it?" I asked Doreen as we went over to the little cottage we were to share. She was wiser.

"Don't you see, Nairobi, he's in a very awkward situation. The met officer is a b-minded old regular who knows Regulations inside out. Met officers don't have to take on extra duties, because in large stations they keep watches, and he won't do a thing. The army officer just about justifies his existence, but is not really under Rob's orders. Joan, your predecessor, thought he should do the catering but he flatly refused. He doesn't get on with Rob. That leaves us. Rob has to persuade us to co-operate, or recognize that he can't run the station!"

I looked around my new quarters. For this one night I was to share with Doreen. We had inherited a Seychellois maid and she had unpacked for me. My large photos of Peter and of Sheba were set up beside the bed; my school hairbrushes laid out on the dressing table, clean uniforms hung in my wardrobe. A door led direct to a bathroom. Space, storage, comfort, and – after tomorrow, when the other room became vacant – privacy. I counted my blessings and climbed into bed. But the darkness and depression descended again. I felt I was walking along a cliff edge, an abyss of mental illness was clutching at me, dragging me down.

I could not sleep but kept questioning myself. Would I be up to all the strains and pressures which would be put on me? I knew nothing about accounts, even less about catering; I was not sure how easy either Rob or Doreen would be to work with. I felt totally alone.

Doreen was fast asleep. I took up shirt and skirt and crept out on to the veranda, where I pulled them on. Barefoot, I walked towards the swimming pool, and beyond it, to the cliff edge overlooking the sea. It was a beautiful night, the full moon shining a path across the bay to the fringe of palm trees, making even our motley collection of tin and thatched roof buildings look romantic. There were no glimmer of artificial light anywhere. I felt an almost tangible presence, as if someone was taking me by the hand. The way was dark, but there was help. For the next four years I clutched that hand hard and frequently. I often wondered if it was my father's.

The next day I set off at dawn, this time with a truck, driver and the cooks' shopping list to collect the rations. In the cool weather the Seychelles was supposed to be a paradise. Its picture postcard palm trees tumbled over deserted beaches; coconuts fell at one's feet; bananas flourished; the shallow warm sea was full of fish; nobody need work. All this I had been told.

It contained elements of truth. For a start the whole island was permeated with the sickly sweet smell of vanilla, only a little of which could be exported owing to the shortage of shipping.

Mahé was indeed a very beautiful island, at that time quite undeveloped, although adjusted to providing for the needs of visiting seamen. In my inexperience, I was astonished to see, that first morning, that its major industry seemed to be the oldest occupation of them all. The main street was red light area, lined with picturesque, old-fashioned colonial houses, each with a different sign: "Paradis de Demoiselles", "Jardin des Femmes" and other seductive titles. Although the sun was only just rising, the girls sat in their windows combing their hair. Even from the truck I could see that each girl was totally different from the one next door.

The mixed history of the Islands had resulted in an extraordinary miscegenation. When French pirates arrived at the beginning of the eighteenth century, the Islands were uninhabited. The French brought in Negro slaves and French planters; Indian and Chinese traders followed. After the Napoleonic Wars, the British had taken over. Since then there had been time for the melting pot to melt. In the same family Negroid, European, and Chinese features would appear. At our mess gates there was a very black family, among them a toddler with curly red hair.

The only colouring I did not see was blonde. I was very fair and when later I went to the barber for a haircut, he asked me what bleach I was using to achieve such a colour. "None," I replied. He walked round me several times as I sat in his chair; took up a strand of my hair and examined it closely, shook his head, and refused even to cut it. I asked Doreen to do it; she was called on duty in the middle of the job, and for days one side of my hair was longer than the other.

As we drove along, the RAF driver told me about his time on the island. The only thing one could not buy easily was food. There were no cattle on the island and no butchers. Everyone lived on fish. Fish was now getting expensive as no one organized the fishermen to catch more. Potatoes were no longer imported so bread fruit was substituted. Bread fruit was also going up in price. The windows of the little shops we passed displayed the most extraordinary mixture of goods: vast corsets, beflowered hats, buttoned gloves and boots, long shoe horns, the flotsam of some cheap European emporium a generation or more out of date.

When we arrived at the army depot, the supply officer was in his office, a tiny cabin in the huge warehouse. He did not look up as I came in, saluted, and said good morning. He took the list I handed him, still without looking at me and without replying to my greeting.

"Why have you applied for two hundred and fifty when your strength is only fifty?" he asked.

"Because it will be two hundred and fifty tomorrow!" I replied.

"Then apply tomorrow!"

At first I did not think he had noticed that I was different from my predecessor. The same old argument was being continued. He handed back my order cut down to a fifth.

"We have two Cats in, one without maintenance crew – so we are seventy-five."

"That's what you should have asked for! I'm not changing anything now!" He put his head down and started to write.

"But you *have* changed it, you've changed it to fifty!"

He did not answer.

"Are you really going to let the RAF fly hungry?" Remembering Rob's words, I tried hard to make my voice light and pleading. He looked up for the first time. He had pale, shifty brown eyes and a Hitler forelock tumbling across his forehead.

"You're new here, aren't you? Well, I'll let you have seventy-five rations this time. But don't try anything on again!"

"I *am* new to this job," I confessed, pasting what I hoped was a helpless woman smile on my face. "Tell me, how do we cook for two hundred and fifty men, with two cooks, if the food arrives after the men do?"

"That's your problem, lady, not mine".

Four hours later I was inspecting the lunch for seventy men. I was appalled by the food and not surprised at the language the men used about it. The butter was rancid, the biscuits full of weevils, the jam crystallized, the bully beef post-dated and disgusting. The cheese came out of huge tins blue with mould. The cooks told me they dumped about a quarter of the rations daily. We officers managed somehow – we had fish at every meal, served with breadfruit and fried bananas, all of which we paid for on our mess bills. The men had not the funds to buy in similar food.

That evening while on duty, I looked through our files to see when the last boat had come in. You can learn a lot from cypher office files. Stores had been received only the previous week. Next day I was down at the ration depot again.

"The food you gave us yesterday was time-expired," I stated, careful to keep my voice pleasant. "We had to dump much of it. Do you think you can find us something better today?" I gave him another smile.

"Lady, I have been running ration depots for thirty years. Stores go out in the same order as they came in."

"But that means you always hand out bad food, and keep the good food until it goes bad!"

"First in, first out is the only way to run a depot. If you don't like it, take your order somewhere else." He went on writing.

In the long ago days of the phoney war a giant stockpile of food had been built up. After four years in a tin shed in the tropics the stockpile had reached deterioration point. Complaints went out, more food was sent in, but there was still plenty of decaying food in blown tins available, so the fresh food never reached us. When fresh meat had been flown in from Mombasa, the army officer had refused to distribute it the evening it arrived and by next morning, without refrigeration, it was inedible. Had it been issued on arrival we could have eaten one meal immediately and cooked sufficient for at least two more. The cook added: "If you boil fresh beef in sea-water, it will last a week. We have plenty of sea-water!"

Even this problem paled into insignificance with the next event – the realization of the premonition I'd had on arrival. It was my first experience of operational tragedy. That afternoon I was on duty when the air radio signal called. I picked up the receiver. It was the first of the Catalinas we were expecting.

"This is Z209 calling Glamour. Are you receiving me? This is Z209 calling Glamour. Are you receiving me?"

"Glamour receiving you loud and clear! Glamour receiving you loud and clear!" I replied. And clear it was, there was a stillness in the air.

"You're the new one, honey, and I'm receiving you loud and clear too." The voice was softly Canadian, caressing and yet amused. "My position is…" He gave his position and repeated it. I checked it back as I wrote it on the blackboard, then stuck a pin in the huge map which was mounted on the wall. Thirty miles out, we should sight him in less than ten minutes.

"I'm coming right in to see you now, honey, so get that launch on stand-by. ETA…" The line went dead. I tried to raise him. No answer. I shouted to the airman in the office behind me to fetch Rob. In a few seconds he was beside me, twirling nobs and pressing buttons. He sent for the signals officer; the machinery was working perfectly. We stood on that veranda uselessly pressing buttons, shouting: "Glamour calling, come in Z209" again and again. There never was any reply. We never knew what happened to Z209, the softly-spoken pilot and his crew.

It was ten years before I heard of the Bermuda triangle. There in the South Indian Ocean we had a triangle all our own; in the few months I was there half a dozen planes disappeared in a similar fashion, two while I was talking to them. Some said they must have flown into the sea, others that shipping or even submarines shot them down. The possibility of some kind of electrical storm operating at the low level at which they were flying was not mentioned. We never had funerals, or even memorial services, when there were no bodies. Once the signals had been sent reporting the men missing, they were never mentioned again.

On my first weekend, on the Saturday evening, I was tidying up my room when a Roll Royce flying the Union Jack swept into the station past our bungalow and parked near mess building. A man climbed out of the car. I recognized him immediately although I had not seen him since I was a child – he had been one of my father's junior officers in the First World War and then later in the administrative service. To my surprise, I heard him ask for me. Apparently among the letters we had brought over was one from Lady Moore telling of my father's death and saying that I needed looking after. He had come down personally to take me back to supper with his family. He too had a daughter stranded at Government House by the war when she should have been in education.

"I'm awfully sorry, but I'm on duty this evening – but I would love to come another time!" I was shouting over the monsoon wind. Doreen appeared at the cypher office window above us,

"Do go!" she said. "I`ll cover for you. You never seem to go out!" She was right, I was usually far too tired by the time I had finished all I had to do.

So I went up to another colonial government house, past the large rooms for entertaining on the ground floor to the family rooms on the first, with wide verandas overlooking the sea some hundreds of yards away. The governor took me to one corner of the veranda from which he had a clear view of our mess and could see whether our flag was flying. His view of the Catalinas was blocked by a new building I had not noticed before. At that moment, Lady Logan arrived with her daughter Jay.

"You won't remember me!" she said.

"I do. When you visited us at our Mombasa house you sang for us. I've always remembered it. It was a full moon that night, and you sang so beautifully."

"And what did I sing?" Was she testing my memory, or had she really forgotten?

"Au Claire de la Lune – you sang all three verses!" I said, and suddenly started crying as I remembered my father taking me on his knee to translate the words. She noticed at once.

"Oh my dear, I am sorry… Can I get you a drink or anything?"

"Would you… would you sing it again for me? Would you mind…?" Was I being impertinent to ask such a favour?

"My dear girl, I'll be delighted to sing it for you."

The arches from the veranda led through to their sitting room and Lady Logan went to her grand piano. And once again the beautiful clear voice rang out over the Indian Ocean and I cried my eyes out as I remembered my father. Then I dried my eyes, accepted a strong gin, and followed them into supper. They wanted to adopt me much as the Moores had done, and were kindness itself. But I only visited them once more after that – life became too hectic on the station.

The next day I went to inspect the new buildings I had seen from Government House. They were in fact on the sea front next door to us. This was to be Combined Headquarters, spacious new offices to be shared by the three services. The naval officer in charge (NOIC) had already moved in. Like Rob, he was a Kenyan and a family friend but I was gratified that he did not recognize me. He showed me the underground operations room with the huge maps, for the next phase of the war. Off it was the windowless cypher room which could not be occupied until the air-conditioning plant arrived. (Strictly speaking, cypher offices on the ground floor had to be windowless to stop people peering in.) The RAF was not to move in until this happened. I laughed and told him the story of TME's air-conditioning.

"There's a spare office on the first floor next door to my office, and your CO's. We could put cyphers there temporarily." He led me upstairs. It was a splendid corner office overlooking the bay.

"This would be splendid!" I enthused. "I hope the air-conditioning never arrives!"

"Wait until the hot weather. Tell me, how should we furnish the cypher office? What kind of tables, what heights?"

"Where will you get the fitting from?" I asked

"The locals make them. They are wonderful craftsmen and can make anything from nothing – but they do need careful direction."

We spent a happy half hour measuring the room out, marking on the wall where the plugs should go, the safe, the desks, all the other equipment. About ten days later Rob came into the old cypher office. I was banging away on the machine, and did not notice his hurt look.

"NOIC has just phoned. He says you agreed to move into an upstairs office and it's now ready. He wants us all to go over and inspect it. I thought we were going to wait for the right equipment."

What a fool I had been. Of course Rob was reluctant to move from his own kingdom – in Combined Ops he would be at best second, possibly third down the list.

"I'm sorry, Rob, I didn't realize he thought I was acting officially. He happens to be a family friend, and I like new building sites."

"Quite so, but in your hurry to move have you thought what it will be like, cyphers over there, pay office over here? You won't be able to do accounts while on cypher watch any more!"

Doreen looked up from bringing the cypher imprest up to date. She needed glasses for close work and pushed them on to her forehead.

"Thank God for that, Rob. When there's a flap on and cyphers are busy, it's hell having the pay people underfoot."

"So you're in on this too?" he asked.

"Certainly not," said Doreen, "I've never heard it mentioned before, but I do long for more space!"

"And you haven't seen the office?"

"No!"

"Well, you'd better come with me, Doreen, and see what you do think!"

Twenty minutes later, I watched them come back as I stood by the pasting table. Rob limped along purposefully, his hurt expressed even in his walk. Doreen was almost dancing with delight.

"Nairobi, that man's a miracle. He's fitted out the office exactly right. There's a proper pasting table, a good light for the book desk, and plenty of room for three machines... and just the right amount of room for the safe. And Rob says we can move next week."

I look round to ask Rob if he approved, but he had disappeared into his office.

"And I've already offended my CO without meaning to," I sighed. No doubt it helped prepare him for the far bigger offence I was to commit.

# Chapter 13
## Flaps and Food

The Naval Officer in charge was a lonely man and had an even smaller mess than ours. In the new offices, he had splendid maps on which to plot his convoys, and since this information was obviously top-secret they were covered by lockable screens. Whenever I was on duty, he would bring his tea tray to share with me, and then we would go together to look at the maps. It helped me greatly to know where the convoys were, as there our squadrons would also be, and I could foretell when flaps would be upon us.

Flaps were always in my mind. More flaps meant more men to feed. The army supply officer grew crankier. The island was full of eggs, chickens, fish, bananas and breadfruit, but because we were being issued with time-expired bully beef and dried peas consisting of green shells full of weevils, he would not allow any local purchasing orders.

My immediate reaction when I saw a flap on the horizon was: "How am I going to feed them?" I must have said this once too often to NOIC, for one day he asked, "What are your numbers? In men days a month?"

I took up a pencil to work them out. He looked over my shoulder:

"About fifty all the time, up to five hundred when there's a flap on. Say ten days a month maximum at four hundred. Flaps increasing all the time," I said.

"Mmm... fifty times thirty plus four hundred times ten – five thousand five hundred man days – not much more than a destroyer. I have to carry enough to refuel any naval ship for six weeks. At the moment we're trying to build up to three times that amount. We can easily take you on," he replied.

I had not thought of this solution and could hardly believe it. "Can you keep it up – we may well be increasing?" I asked.

He sat on the high bench near my machine and looked down at me, amused at my doubt.

"No one can guarantee anything in wartime. Put it this way. Your entire rations for six months are equivalent to my minimum reserve ration strength. At the moment we hold well in excess. Were we to be really besieged, like Malta, then we might all end up eating the army's hump. But if that happens, yours truly will be out in those lagoons organizing the fishing!" I remembered that he was well known as a big game fisherman.

It was two days before I found a suitable moment to speak to Rob. Always a poor delegator, he spent much time bustling round after everyone else, so he rarely had time to think about major decisions. I chose a serene moment after a fishy but passable Sunday lunch.

"Rob, why don't we ask the navy to feed us ?"

"Couldn't do it, my dear girl. You don't understand how the services work. Anyway, NOIC wouldn't dream of it, not this one. I told you, this is not the place to start reforming the world. You have to stick to the system, u/s* though it may be!"

I went back to NOIC dispirited.

"Commander Ferguson, I would like to accept your offer, but someone else will have to talk my CO into it." He had covered his maps as I came in, and opened them up again when he saw it was me. He went on sticking in coloured pins.

"Never mind, circumstances may help!"

I glanced over his shoulder at the bunches of pins – all those convoys on the high seas, approaching our part of the Indian Ocean. Convoys meant sweeps, and sweeps meant flaps.

The next evening three hundred and fifty men flew in with twenty-five Catalinas to sweep ahead of the ships. The supply officer had refused me rations in the morning because the men had not arrived. He refused them again that evening because I sent the order down after 6 p.m. I could not send it earlier because our two trucks were ferrying the men

---

* u/s stood for unserviceable - a very usual word in RAP speak!

from the port to the station. This refusal stimulated even Rob into action. Scarlet with anger, he jumped into the station car. Rations arrived at 8 p.m. We could smell the bad meat throughout the camp as the tins were opened. Four hundred men went to bed hungry.

The next morning a hundred and fifty took off on operations after a breakfast of hardtack biscuits. At least tinned jam kept well. The oatmeal we had been issued as porridge was so full of weevils that the cooks said it would jump out of the saucepans.

That same day, at a late breakfast after we had seen the crews off, Rob kept looking at me. I could see he was searching for words. At last he said: "June, did NOIC actually offer to provision us, or is it just one of your bright ideas?"

"It was he who suggested it, Rob. I was grumbling about the situation, and he came out with this!"

Ten minutes later, as I sat in the old cypher office checking the account books, I saw Rob leave in the direction of NOIC's office; his cap was pressed down on the springy red curls and his cocky stride showed his determination. I phoned Doreen, who was in the cypher office, and told her that I would be late in relieving her. I wanted to keep out of the way.

The next morning at dawn NOIC himself was at the naval supply depot when I arrived in our truck with our senior cook. We could not believe our eyes: whole sides of frozen meat from their cold storage room, sides of bacon and ham, crates of condensed milk, jars of coffee, bags of oats, tins of Kenya butter, great round cheddar cheeses, sacks of white flour, biscuits, tins of fruit, everything on my list and much that was not poured into our waiting truck. The naval supply petty officer then apologized, the notice had been too short to bake us fresh bread for today, but from tomorrow on there would be fresh bread every morning. Could we phone him when we knew our numbers were increasing? Commander Ferguson stepped in, this information could not go on the open phone line but he was aware of the situation and would keep the petty officer informed.

The cook was laughing all the way home. More food meant more work, but he called on volunteers to help out and for once there were more volunteers than he could handle. For once, more work was good news.

The flap continued and it was two days before I found time to inspect a meal. The senior cook came out to accompany me. He was still smiling. The long room, open on one side to the garden, was crowded with hot sweaty men queuing at the counter. We worked our way to the corner at the far end, where our locals always congregated in a group apart from the visitors. When they saw me, they stood up and started clapping. The visiting crews joined in. They kept it up until tears streamed down my face and I hurried over to thank NOIC.

After that I inspected meals only once a week. The food was now good enough for some wit to come out with the old chestnut in reply to "Any complaints?"

"Yes, miss, but it's not the food, it's my trousers, they're too tight!"

An enormous burden had been lifted from my mind, but another one replaced it. I had to act as pay master. Paying some fifty men their full entitlement each fortnight was little problem. The pay sergeant, a trainee accountant in civvy street, made up the paybooks; we went together to the bank to collect the money, he counted out the amounts due and stacked it in piles on each pay book. The men paraded in front of us, the sergeant called the names, I checked the amount and handed it over, the man signed his book and the register. We could process a man a minute – a piece of cake in RAF terms.

The problems arose when there were several hundred who wanted to be paid, when there was no time to hand in the pay books in advance, when they wanted their pay in a combination of East African shillings, Indian rupees and Madagascan francs. One disastrous day the parade lasted six hours. As it had to be held in the dining room we had to pack up for lunch and start up again afterwards. My sergeant thought to organize three separate parades, one for each currency. This the mobile units did not like, they did not want to parade three times.

It was rare that our books balanced exactly because of the problems in working out exchange rates to the last cent. When we checked the currency after our first complex pay parade, we had three shillings too much. I put it in an envelope labelled "Too much". On the next parade we had less than a shilling too little left. I added the words "Too little" to the envelope and took a shilling from the envelope to make up the difference. The amount in the envelope was always small, less than a pound, nor did I ever need to augment it. This system saved hours of work.

All went well until the auditors came over, a wing commander/professional accountant. As was customary, he got to the cash box with the CO's keys before I had time to remove the envelope.

"What is the meaning of this?" he shouted, shaking with fury as he brandished the envelope in front of me. I explained the difficulties.

"I have never heard of such a thing! You always account for the last cent, do you hear me!" I thought the next island could probably hear him, but kept my peace.

"If it takes you six hours, it takes you six hours, and that teaches you to be more careful next time."

"Sir, the problem only occurs when there's a flap on, and then there just is not six hours!"

"There is always six hours; a little bit of midnight oil never did anyone any harm!"

"Sir, when a flap is on, I'm up every other night as it is!"

"What do you mean, up every other night?"

"I'm one of two cypher officers, sir!"

"Cypher officers are not supposed to be pay officers!"

"Quite so, sir!"

There was a pause as he took in the situation. His voice was kinder when he spoke again.

"What else do you do, may I ask – cypher officer, imprest holder, pay officer?"

"The catering, sir!"

"Ah, so that's why the food is so much better."

"Thank you, sir, but it's…"

"No buts, girl. I'll see if we can lighten your load when I return to HQ. There's no need to mess up the accounts just because you're a cypher officer doing the catering!"

I summonsed up my courage to ask: "How do I solve the problem of paying in three different currencies, sir?"

He looked out of the window, at the Catalinas bobbing gently up and down on the waves and the deep blue sea meeting the lighter blue sky in the distance. The monsoon was over now and the swell was at its lowest. I wondered if he had heard me.

"You treat it as the banks used to treat the issue of foreign currency." I had no experience of pre-war currency exchange, but was reluctant to admit I had been only just sixteen when the war started. "You pay in the local currency, and see that your books balance to the last cent. That keeps me happy. As a separate operation, buy a suitable amount of francs or rupees from the bank, and get someone else to run a bureau de change on the side. The bank might lend you a clerk for an hour or two to do just that. I'll have a word…" He went over to the phone and started cranking.

"That would be excellent, sir. I usually pay the second and fourth Fridays, but during a flap we have at least one extra parade a week and that's when we have to change currency. May I go back to the cypher office now – my colleague has been there all day."

"Yes, but one other thing. I am not having you collecting money from the bank. In future, the sergeant goes, with an armed policeman and one of the male officers. Not you, you understand? I will not have women at risk."

I did not see there was much risk from an armed hold-up in the Seychelles, and we had no policemen on our strength, but I knew better than to argue. It would have to be the met officer or the signals chappie who accompanied the sergeant; each would argue he was too busy. I wondered who would win, and whether they could produce a gun among them.

The Islands were surprisingly free of tropical diseases – no malaria, no hook worm, no sand fly fever. We all knew that there was leprosy around, and that lepers were confined to one of the smaller islands. My own health remained the same as before: the chronic dysentery I had brought with me and prickly heat. As the hot season came upon us and the atmosphere grew hot and humid, the strawberry red rash reappeared all over my body and the itchiness drove me to distraction, and eventually to the doctor.

There was no RAF doctor and we used a civilian one, an old resident of the island. A grey-haired, portly, courteous man, he toyed with a paper knife as I spoke. He surveyed me carefully, making me aware how unattractive my uniform was. I wore a very thin, short-sleeved khaki shirt tucked into a drill skirt, khaki ankle socks and black sandals. Eventually he spoke.

"You must not mind me saying this to you, my dear. I am an old man, a married man, and I have a great deal of experience. Now what

I am going to say…" I fidgeted in my chair. What was it all about? "I think you should leave off your petticoat! The fewer clothes you wear the less itchy you will be!"

How could I tell him that I did not possess a petticoat? But he did give me one useful bit of advice: after a bath, a rub-down with spirits, any spirits would do – eau-de-cologne or meths or rum all hardened the skin and relieved the itching. He was right, it worked, but only for an hour or so at a time. I took to carrying a bottle of eau-de-cologne round with me. Fortunately the local shops seemed to hold a good stock of German eau-de-cologne, 4711.

The great advantage of my lifestyle was that it left me no time to think. Every minute of every day had to be planned to cram in the jobs that had to be done. I saw little of the island, crossing only twice to Beau Vallon in my entire stay, and only once visiting the Eastern beach where now the new runway juts into the sea. Apart from Beau Vallon, there was nowhere to go, no dance hall, no other messes to visit, no cinema. I knew that the various Jardins des Femmes were doing a thriving trade and that VD was rife but that was not my problem.

Apart from our work, the main pressures on us two WAAFs came from a different source. Many young aircrew, highly strung and lonely, sought a sympathetic female ear, and often something more than an ear, to reduce the tensions building up in them. This pressure was exacerbated by the casualty list. I learned for the first time that, in war, sex and death go together. Or is it that the fear of death makes sex more desirable? For some flights the death rate was as high as one aircraft every two months. As each squadron had only six aircraft, this meant the casualty rate was around a hundred per cent a year. We were not encouraged to express casualties in such statistics, but the young men were fully aware of them. Many were bitter to be so much at risk in such a forgotten corner of the war. These were no longer the few to whom the many owed so much; they were a younger generation of boys just out of school and training colleges in Canada. Most of them had yet to develop the stamina and endurance that flying Catalinas in adverse circumstances demanded – very different qualities from the courage and spontaneity needed by a fighter pilot.

The strain was made worse by the weather. The short cool season was soon over. Sweat dripped from us and eau-de-cologne friction no longer sufficed to prevent prickly heat. We all tended to make more mistakes. One day in early October when the monsoon was trying to change, the worst mistake of all occurred. At full moon of the equinox tide, when the swell was high, we had a flap on. Two squadrons of Cats were coming in. Doreen and I stood on the balcony, hearts in mouths, as they bounced one after the other on the heaving waves. Doreen was wearing the headphones and talking them down, I was using binoculars to spot them and writing arrival times on the blackboard against the call signs and ETAs. Six arrived from Dar es Salaam, only five from Diego Suarez, all of them circling us, making a north-west approach to face the changing monsoon, which at that moment was blowing strongly across the tip of the island from the south-east. Each in turn bounced down in front of us, and followed the waiting launch to its allotted buoy.

We scanned the sky anxiously for the twelfth plane. Doreen picked him up before I did. He came in roaring low over the mess, and instead of circling for a sea approach from the north-west, he made a direct approach to the buoys, landing with the wind instead of against it. The great plane smacked the waves too fast, waddled for thirty seconds down into a trough and up again, then wind and waves turned her tail over nose. As her back hit the water, she broke in two. My hand found the alarm button and the whole station sprang into life. Although by land we were a mile from the jetty, our launch was out before she settled on the water, the naval launch seconds after ours. We could see heads bobbing about, and men in the launch throwing lifebelts. This was the deep water anchorage and sharks abounded, drawn by the refuse discarded by ships. There had been twenty men on board; eight came out alive, all badly injured. Six bodies were recovered. It was one small incident in a terrible war but the worst accident we had had on the island.

As always in the Tropics, we had to have the funerals within twenty-four hours. There was to be one grave with all twelve names on it. In the heat of the next afternoon we slow-marched down to the cathedral, our dead preceding us in one of the trucks. Everyone was there, NOIC with a naval party, the governor, the doctor, the directors of education and of cable and wireless, the senior police officer, even my old sparring partner, the army supply officer.

On the way back I visited the eight cheerless survivors in the tiny civilian hospital. The pilot was a tall, loosely built, blond-haired

Canadian on his first operational tour. He was miserably homesick, took the heat badly, and on an earlier visit Doreen and I had already marked him down as a case of overstrain. When, two days after the accident, Rob told him he was responsible for the twelve deaths and would probably be court-martialled, he lay in the hot little hospital ward, his head bandaged, sobbing uncontrollably. The nuns who looked after him were in despair.

Back at the office I sat down and wrote twelve letters to the bereaved parents, describing the funeral to them, trying to make out that each man had died a heroic death on active service, not in a terrible blunder. They were difficult letters to write; I had to keep them official in case there were girlfriends back home who would hate to read about the party we had last time the plane had called. Rob had asked me to write the letters as he had so much else to do with investigating and reporting the crash, but in the end I wrote them as if they were from him and persuaded him to sign them.

A few days later Doreen told me my posting had come through; I was to leave on the next Catalina to Mombasa en route for Mediterranean Allied Air Force Headquarters in Italy. The signal had ended up on Rob's desk. He sent for me.

"I want you to take the papers about the crash for me. There must be a court-martial!"

Rob had set up a board of enquiry at once. All kinds of disturbing facts came to life. Regulations were that life-jackets had to be worn throughout every flight. As they were hot and cumbersome garments, they were often discarded. The fact that they had not been worn even for landing had probably accounted for at least some of the deaths. It was important to establish why they had not been worn.

In the RAF the pilot is always the captain of the plane. This pilot was a nineteen-year-old, quite unable to control the seasoned crew allocated to him, let alone give orders to the spare crew who were hitching a ride on his plane. Moreover, the pilot of the spare crew was a very experienced man and in a better organized system could have trained the younger pilot. Remarks kept slipping out from the survivors, which showed that Diego Suarez Squadron was an unhappy one. Yet how could any pilot make such a basic error as to land downwind?

Pilot error was the cause of the accident, lack of discipline had added to the casualty list. Rob speeded up his preliminary report, determined to send it back with me. "Mind you give it to Group Captain Douglas-Hamilton himself," he said, "not the personnel officer."

Before I left, I went to say goodbye to the doctor and enquired after the pilot.

"He'll never fly again, and the sooner he can get back to Canada and out of the service the better. He's already scarred for life, but who knows what these bright young men will do with him? In my view, the ordeal of a court-martial will kill him."

"Will he recover, physically?"

"Physically, he has had a severe blow on the head, and we know very little about the brain. He should recover sufficiently to lead a normal life, if he can get over his feelings of guilt. But if things go on as they are now..." He shrugged his shoulders.

My other goodbye call was to the governor. Government House was not as near to our mess as the one at Nairobi had been, but it was only a five-minute stroll away. I felt guilty that I had responded so little to their kindness and invitations, managing only one dinner with them during my entire stay. We met at funerals and church services. Now when I called to say goodbye, the governor's daughter ushered me into his study. He made us both sit down and I had to tell him why I had been so busy, indeed what I had found to do, on the Islands.

When I told them, he commented: "You sound just like your father in the last war. One work horse breeds another!"

I packed the fat file Rob gave me in the bottom of my suitcase, and moved into Doreen's room for the night so my replacement could go straight into a room of her own. On a windy day in early October I flew out of the Seychelles forever. At least I thought forever.

Then in 2003 we were visiting my sister in Kenya and we thought we would go over and look at the old place. There is now a landing strip built out over the sea. Our little hotel, Combined Forces HQ, and HMS Seychelles and the naval messes have all disappeared, to be replaced by a long row of oil tanks. The cathedral has also gone, to be replaced by another, more modern building. Neither the plaque in the cathedral nor the one in the graveyard have survived. The graveyard has become a car park. More surprisingly, tourist literature makes no mention of the Second World War. The Japanese subs might never have existed. Yet the Seychelles' participation in the First World War is carefully and accurately recorded. The Seychellois people made a great contribution to the Carrier Corps, where the British in Kenya were fighting the Germans in Tanganyika (now Tanzania), working as medical orderlies, clerks, caterers, mechanics, supervisors of all kinds. In the second world war they were welcoming and helpful throughout in our endeavours to keep the Indian Ocean open and The Islands free of Japanese occupation. They should be proud of their record rather than try to ignore it.

# Chapter 14
## Mess in Madagascar

We flew to Mombasa via Diego Suarez, in the north-east corner of the island of Madagascar, home of the unhappy squadron whose Catalina had crashed. All kinds of rumours had been circulating about this station. Now I was able to see it for myself. We touched down in a sheltered cove where tiny waves lapped the sandy, palm-fringed beach. The mess and station were situated on a cliff high above, where the monsoons cooled the hot buildings. A jeep, one of the first I had seen, bumped us up the hill amid a forest of flowering shrubs. It looked more like an idyllic holiday hotel than an active air force station in time of war.

The idyll stopped at the station gates. Offices and mess were chaotic. The commander was a tour-expired man. Tour-ex was often a polite way of describing a man who had been so stretched by dicing with death on dangerous flying sorties that he no longer cared what he did. Life seemed meaningless and ordinary social restraints no longer applied. As the war dragged on year after year, the RAF accumulated a number of these characters. They were often posted as officers commanding to remote stations. Most were forbidden operational flying, and found the lack of danger boring. Too often, drink was the solution. In this mess, life had become one long sodden party. This was particularly disastrous in a unit receiving very young commonwealth pilots on their first operational posting.

Moreover, discipline was openly flouted on every possible occasion, often by the CO himself. Matters had come to a head at a certain parade organized by the army. The night before the parade there had been a party in the RAF mess. The CO, sweating from too much alcohol, had taken off his shirt and some wit had painted all his decorations on his naked torso. The next day the parade started early to avoid the midday heat; the wing commander appeared on parade shirtless, the coloured ink still gleaming brightly on a bronzed and hairy chest. The army commander, a conventional regular, had him arrested.

All kinds of problems arose. Did the army have the authority to arrest the commanding officer of another service? Who should take over authority in the RAF station? The second-in-command agreed to take responsibility only if the CO remained on his own station; he could occupy the sick bay. The army said they would only release him if two army officers accompanied him until he left the island.

All the Catalinas were away on a flap, so there was no way to fly the wing commander back to the mainland. When our Catalina flew in for a stopover, the army commander sent for our pilot and said he was to evacuate the wing-commander. The pilot said his Catalina was already fully laden; otherwise he would not have night-stopped. The army officer insisted on seeing the passenger list and suggested that I should be left on Diego until the next flight. The pilot refused, saying his instructions were to deliver me to Mombasa for onward transmission to Italy. Officers proceeding on active duty always took precedence over all other categories. The colonel had difficulty in accepting that a woman could be on active service. The pilot refused to accept that the CO was so ill that he needed immediate evacuation.

The next day we were delayed while the discussion continued. Eventually the Catalina took off with me and without the wing commander. I had added another large packet of papers to be delivered to RAFHQ in Nairobi. After a night in the mess at Mombasa, it was gratifying to have a car to meet the dawn flight at what is now Wilson Airport in Nairobi. The group captain was expecting me and ordered coffee before getting down to our debriefing session. I handed over the Diego papers, remembering that the Seychelles ones were in my suitcase in the guardroom. Would he excuse me while I fetched them?

"Don't worry just now," he said glancing through the Diego ones. "I want your opinions first!"

What was happening at Diego? Were things as bad as the army CO reported or was he being officious? The wing commander concerned had a splendid record on active service. I pointed out that we had spent only one night on the station, but it had seemed very disorganized, and none of the usual customs or disciplines were being maintained. Had life-jackets been worn, the recent accident would probably have claimed fewer lives. And should not young pilots be given tuition by experienced pilots when first landing on a high swell?

"You mean nothing like that is happening?"

"I don't think so. It seemed mad to me to have the experienced pilot as a passenger in a fully loaded plane flown by a newcomer when conditions were at their worst."

He opened another file on his desk. I could see the signals about the accident, which Doreen had encyphered a few days earlier. He fired more questions at me, this time about the Seychelles. Why was Rob so keen on a court-martial? Court-martials were serious and time-consuming. If the pilot had shown an error of judgement, he had paid dearly for it.

"I'll get the papers, sir," I said again, "they're in my case."

"No, no, sit down, Miss Watkins, I'll see them later. I want your views on the matter. You were there. Did you know the pilot?"

"Yes, sir. He was very strained and nervous two weeks earlier, on a visit to us. The doctor, a civilian, says he'll never fly again, and from the medical viewpoint thinks he should be discharged as quickly and quietly as possible."

"Did you visit him afterwards?"

"Oh yes, sir. He was very distressed, sobbing, saying he had killed his friends. He had severe head injuries, as well as concussion, and was overwhelmed by his feelings of guilt."

"So we're talking about a man who will be invalided out in any case?"

"It would seem so, sir. The doc's point was that hanging around for a court-martial and all the extra strain and suspense was the worst possible way to convalesce. He said that after serious head injuries you need a long spell of peace and quiet."

Somehow the whole morning disappeared in a question and answer session. Finally the group captain stood up.

"We'll adjourn for lunch! Come over to the mess and meet the AOC. He wants to talk to you." I was already feeling flattered by the way I had been treated that morning. It was a heady feeling, the feeling that someone had sought my opinion, trusted my judgement. Now I was to be even more flattered.

"I've heard glowing reports about you, young woman," said the air commodore. "Yours is the only station in my experience to move its catering arrangements from the army to the navy. I hear you have achieved the best-fed station in the Indian Ocean, and other catering officers are asking why they cannot switch as well!" He turned to the lunch table. "I hope our lunch comes up to your standards!"

I had left Mombasa before breakfast was served and the sight of all those fresh salads made me feel famished.

"It looks delicious, sir. I had almost forgotten about salads!"

"I gather you are on your way up to Italy?"

"Yes, sir. I haven't been to movements yet, so I don't know when."

"Quite soon, as far as I can remember," said the group captain. "We have put you down to escort another batch of airwomen up to ME. Let me see, that will be on Thursday's flying boat from Kisumu – the day after tomorrow. What's your mother think about this?" He had not mentioned my mother the whole morning.

"I haven't seen her yet, sir; and she doesn't know I'm coming or going. She's up at Molo for a few days. I rang home from the airport and my sister suggested I hire a car and go to join her, but now…" I did not think I would have time. Molo was up in the highlands, the other side of the great rift valley, more than one hundred and fifty miles from Nairobi on rutted, unsurfaced roads. It was normally considered an eight-hour drive.

"I think you had better leave straight away," said the group captain, "or you'll hardly see her. I'll drive you down now to hire a car."

On the way down, he asked: "What are you going to do after the war?"

"I always hoped to go to Oxford, sir. But now I don't know whether I'll make it."

"That's exactly right! Of course you'll make it. I only asked because if ever there's anything I can do to help, I hope you'll let me know. When it comes to finding jobs, or even university places, references are useful, particularly when you know they will be good ones!"

So it was that at half-past-two on a dusty October afternoon, I pointed the nose of an ancient Chevrolet out of Nairobi up the new road being constructed by the Italian prisoners of war. On the edge of the escarpment I paused to look at the Rift Valley, that great gash across the face of Africa, with the strange volcanoes rising from its bed. The new road became the old road, a corrugated murram track leading steeply down its slippery side. I drove as fast as I dared, rattling and skidding on the stony surface, enveloped in clouds of dust whenever I met another vehicle. I drove past Naivasha, past the great pink cloud of flamingoes on Lake Elementeita, on through Nakuru – what an ugly cow town that place was – and across rolling hill country, climbing gently out of the valley, on either side extensive farms with fenced fields, thorough bred livestock, and large areas planted with one crop.

The journey seemed endless but it was only seven when, as dusk deepened into night, I bounced up the Gray's long farm track. The farmhouse nestled long and low into a hillside. The Gray's were some of Kenya's most enterprising pioneers, they had introduced cheese making to the country. My mother had nursed him back to health in 1914. It had never occurred to me that they would not be pleased to see me, arriving late, unannounced, and dishevelled. Colonial hospitality did not let me down. There was a warm welcome, a hot bath, a good supper and a spare bed in mother's room – in true Kenya style the spare room was a separate small house in the grounds with its own bathroom and veranda.

The Grays were not rich by any standards, but there was a great attention to detail. Unusually for Kenya, the house was beautifully run; the furnishings looked like a picture in a glossy magazine. The sheets, towels, curtains, covers in each room were carefully matched and co-ordinated, very unusual in those days. I remembered the shabbiness of my own home, Wispers: the worn curtains, the patched sheets stained red by the water, the rugs stiff with mud from the dogs. I was tactless enough to comment to Mother.

"The poor Grays never had any children," said Mother firmly. "A perfect house is a very poor substitute for any woman!" We talked for hours that night; I was beginning to understand how lonely she was. I was still talking when I realized that she had fallen asleep.

The next morning Mother said she would return with me. We decided to leave at midday. By this time I had lost the car keys, and connected the leads across the battery as my father had taught me to do. I set off to a push start – and found the steering was locked. The Chevrolet kept in a straight line and demolished the ornamental gatepost bordering the immaculate garden. While we were surveying the mess – I was more concerned about the car while Mother was apologizing for the gatepost – the house servant came out of our room waving the car keys. Mother never said a word.

Further down the road we ran out of petrol. My efforts at being grown up, responsible, looking after Mother, were not very successful. We arrived at Wispers late and tired. When I unpacked my suitcase I found the papers I should have given to the group captain. I put them on the table to hand over the following day.

I fell asleep on the floor of the big sitting room easily, a happy Sheba warm against me. This was my fourth night of undisturbed sleep, a great luxury for any watch-keeper, and three more stretched ahead. The change of venue each night worried me not at all. I woke up very early thinking about the Canadian pilot, certain that if the court-martial went ahead he would have a total breakdown. Did the group captain want Rob's accident report? If he received it, he had either to allow Rob's request for a court-martial or refuse it. I knew he did not want to allow it; at the same time he did not want to refuse Rob, who would take it hard if his recommendation were not accepted.

If the papers were lost it would delay proceedings for about a month. This might well be time enough to get the pilot back to Canada and sanity. And who knew what might happen in the fortunes of war in that time? Even Rob's opinions had been known to change. I would take the envelope in with me to headquarters, go to say goodbye to the group captain, but only hand it over if he asked for it.

At 6 a.m. the phone rang. I got to it first, before an ashen Ronny who always thought any call at an untoward time would be bad news about her husband Pat. The call was for me. The flight to Kisumu had been cancelled, and we had to leave immediately by road for a two hundred and fifty-mile drive to catch the evening flying boat at Kisumu. The transport would pick me up in one hour's time in Nairobi at a venue of my choosing. I chose the car hire garage. Yes, my movement orders and those for my party would all be on board.

The colour returned to Ronny's face. Richard appeared, sleepy and adorable. He was now two years old, a picture postcard toddler, and immediately made his way up the passage to his grandmother's room. We sisters followed and sat on her bed to share her morning tea.

As I collected my case I saw the huge brown envelope on the table. I picked it up, went out to the long drop lavatory and listened for the thud as it reached the bottom. I was taking a serious risk in deliberately destroying papers, my first ever serious offence; but the weight off my mind was enormous. From the service point of view, I was committing a major crime, yet inside me, I knew I was doing the right thing. It was with a light heart that I patted the disconsolate Sheba, turned the Chev's ignition key into a purring start and waved a cheerful goodbye to Wispers. Next year would see the end of the war and I would be back again. I did not know that never again would I see Wispers as my home.

# Chapter 15
## Journey to Italy

It was a notoriously unreliable way to travel, by road in Kenya in those days, but on this occasion we made it. The two staff cars into which they had crammed six newly recruited WAAFS, two RAF officers and myself rattled and bounced over the corrugated roads, following the route I had so recently driven myself.

The road passed the Gray's farm, climbed through thick forest to an altitude of ten thousand feet, then rolled gently six thousand feet down to Kisumu. We left the highlands with the wide sweeping fields dotted with trees and grazing cattle, and crossed into Luo country, the tribe my mother favoured so much and always recruited to work on her farm. It was one of the most thickly populated areas in the country, the little settlements of mud and grass huts with their euphorbia hedges set close together.

It had been a bad year for rain. One harvest of spindly maize had already been taken; now rain was awaited to plant the next. There were plenty of people about, the men mostly dressed in ragged shorts and shirts, the women clad in a few beads round the waist or a cloth wrapped tight across their breasts. They walked superbly, loads balanced on their heads, babies clamped to their backs. No one here was bent forward under an impossibly heavy load on their backs, as were the women around Nairobi.

We arrived dust-covered and shaken up, but on time for the Imperial Airways flying boat, which still maintained a regular service from South Africa to Alexandria. By the autumn of 1944, it was not the case of *if* we won the war, but *when*. It was cheering to think that by the end of this year, the service might be continuing all the way to Southampton. None of us knew how painful and long drawn out the last fighting across Europe would be. I knew only that there was still work to be done in Europe, and I was going to be in at the kill.

This was my second visit to the Grand Hotel at Entebbe, specially built for the Imperial Airways flights. A brilliant green golf course scattered with flame trees stretched down to the lake. The course was famous because it permitted players to remove golf balls from hippo footprints without penalties.

I saw the new recruits into their rooms and was standing by the window of my comfortable room, planning a walk to the lake to watch the big flocks of water birds that congregated there at night, when two of the girls knocked on my door. They needed sanitary towels. No, they had not realized that one very often needed them on long flights, and would I produce some, urgently. In those days, universal vending machines lay in the distant future. We were a long way from the shops, which would in any case be closed. Yes, they had asked the other girls and no one had any with them.

The hotel was not accustomed to women travelling. I went to the desk and asked whether there were any medical supplies. They had nothing. I went to the phone and rang up the government doctor. Fortunately he was in. He did not like being disturbed at home for frivolous reasons, but he would have his orderly send up rolls of cotton wool. No, there was no chance of persuading the chemist to open up and the other shops were all closed. It was not his problem. The girls should think ahead.

I stayed in my room to see what would happen. In about twenty minutes a portly hotel servant in a flowing Arab robe arrived bearing a gleaming brass tray. He bowed before me as if offering me the crown jewels – instead of two large purple rolls of cotton wool. My father had taught me always to look at Africans and try to tell which tribe they came from; when I looked at this man I learned only that he was nearly exploding with suppressed laughter. I dared not catch his eye for I would have exploded too. I grabbed the wool and fled up to the girls' rooms.

"We can't use that stuff!" they screamed.

"I'm afraid that you'll have to!" I said. "No chance of buying anything better before Khartoum, and very little there!"

At Khartoum there was a huge staff car waiting to meet the plane. As I stepped ashore from the launch the chauffeur opened the door and a tall young man in a major's uniform came to meet me. It was Nigel Ready, a neighbour of ours in Kent. Somehow he had heard I was coming through. He had also heard I was going to Europe, and was anxious for me to take a parcel to his fiancée in England. I checked the girls had transport and set off with Nigel, arriving at the hotel in such style and ahead of all the other passengers that it was assumed we were a VIP couple. We were shown up to a magnificent room overlooking the river and the road. It was obviously a case of mistaken identity.

"Look what you've achieved for me!" I said as I stepped onto the balcony.

"I've not seen the rooms before – it is rather good. Pity we can't share it! But I'm engaged and I wouldn't mind betting you've left your heart somewhere. Pick you up in half an hour for dinner?"

"Make that an hour and half!" I said. "I want to do justice to that bathroom and then I have the girls to look after!"

The girls were packed into the smaller rooms in a ground floor annex at the back, two to a room. One of the rooms had had a third bed added, no doubt for me. After my bath I saw the girls into dinner.

Nigel took me to his club for dinner, and afterwards we wandered through the old town to the bazaar. It would be hard to find a place more different from Nairobi. Khartoum was old, mature, historic, stately and sleepy, not full of tin shack streets and cow town excitement like Nairobi. It had wide, shady streets lined with great arched colonial buildings in brick or stone to accommodate the offices of empire. Even bargaining in the twisting alleys of the Arab bazaar was carried on in a dignified manner with none of the brash take-it-or-leave-it shouting of the Nairobi bazaar. We selected presents for his fiancée, a silk dressing gown and a blouse, pretty to wear and light to pack. I told him one of the RAF passengers was going to Blighty and would take the parcel for him. When he heard Europe meant Italy as far as I was concerned, he commented, "Lucky you. You, a chit of a girl, go for the second time into the thick of action, and I, in the regular army, have been stuck here all the war!"

**124**

Back at the hotel, I found the girls had also gone out. I took a stool onto my balcony above the front entrance, and waited for them to come back. There was a full moon; the night was utterly quiet. The moonlight shone on the fast-flowing river and even in that light the blue water showed up distinct from the white. In the garden below me, a snake glided slowly across the grass. There was a rustling. In a minute a mongoose appeared and did a little dance. The snake moved in to strike. The mongoose moved a few steps and danced again. I realized it was leading the snake away from its hole. For twenty minutes I watched the battle between snake and mongoose, Kipling's Riki Tiki Tavi in real life. By the time the mongoose delivered its conclusive blow, I was dripping with sweat, although the night was comparatively cool.

Two taxis drove up and a crowd of girls and men disentangled themselves. I counted carefully, and then recounted. There were only five girls. I dashed downstairs. Yes, one girl had broken off from the party and gone to another nightclub, refusing to return with them. It was after midnight and we had to get up at 4.30 am. I returned anxiously to my balcony; another hour passed with no sign of the missing girl. I visualized reporting to Headquarters in Cairo: "Sorry Ma'am, I lost a girl in Khartoum!"

At last I asked the night porter to get me a taxi so I could go and look for her. He found a watchman to come with me, and I woke one of the girls to show me where they had been. They had gone out, six girls together, to seek entertainment. A taxi had taken them to a nightclub where they had joined up with a party of officers, and after a while they had moved on to another club. The doorman of the second club knew where the missing girl had gone.

When we found her, in the third club, she was drunk but sleepy and amenable to returning quietly – indeed she was glad to see us. The problem came when we had to get her up only two hours after she went to bed. I was thankful to hand a complete set of six girls over at the new base camp in Cairo and to take myself off to the transit camp.

A transit camp was a cheap solution to accommodating the huge number of officers now passing through Cairo. Formerly we had been sent to hotels, now we were put under canvas, four to a tent. I reported to the movements officer that evening and was told that I must expect to wait at least a week for a plane to Naples.

Next day I unpacked a blue uniform, thick stockings, black lace-up walking shoes and black tie – the first time I had worn blues since my father's funeral. I wandered over to ablutions (set in cement huts in the middle of the compound), washed my hair, and started to do my laundry, having done none since leaving the Seychelles. The washing was still unrinsed when my name was called on the tannoy. I was to leave at once for the airport.

After all the hurry the plane did not leave until the afternoon. It was a Dakota, the first I had flown in, fitted with a narrow iron bench down each side. The benches were crowded and very uncomfortable. There was a protuberance behind them which caught one in the back, so in the end I chose to sit on mailbags on the floor.

We stopped in Malta on a wet October evening to refuel – it was still light enough to see the appalling bomb damage and the debris of war strewn around. We were handed packs of dry sandwiches. By the time we reached Naples it was dark and pouring with rain. We drove twenty miles to Caserta and through the palace gates into the courtyard. Here I was dumped with my bag in the dark and wet, and someone pointed out where the WAAF transport left. There was a truck standing there, so I went up to the back and called out, "Is this right for the WAAF mess?"

"June!" a dozen voices called out, and a forest of hands reached down to pull me on board. Inside were A-Watch, who had just come off duty that evening, and Winifred Laws. I was among friends. The WAAF quarters were a commandeered farmhouse with a row of hutments stretching out behind it into an orange grove. Topsy, whom I had not seen since distant TME days, took me in charge, found an empty cubicle for me, and led me back into the farmhouse, this time into the wash kitchen. The wall opposite the boilers had been fitted out with shower units. Three women stood there, stark naked, showering in steaming hot water.

"Ma'am, this is Watkins from Nairobi," Topsy said. I was still wearing my cap and did not know whether to salute a completely naked woman or not. Hastily I pulled it off.

"Quite right, my girl, just what I would have done!" said the group officer.

"Hallo, so it's you!" said another of the naked ladies. It was the squadron officer who had recruited me.

"Thank you, Ma'am, for arranging this posting!" I said. The group officer stopped soaping herself and peered round the edge of the partition at her colleague.

"You mean, this one actually asked to come here?"

"Obviously she doesn't know what she's coming to!" And she gave me a knowing wink.

"And who is your reason?" asked Topsy as she led me away. "The same dishy wing-co?"

"A-Watch, of course!" I replied, but to myself I thought: "He's here and been promoted."

"Liar!" she said.

I changed into my best uniform and did my face with particular care – I might meet Peter that evening. A-Watch had come off duty at 7.30 p.m. and the transport, which had taken us to our quarters, waited to take us back to supper in the men's mess, a big-tented site just below the railway line, which ran in front of the palace. I kept looking and looking but he was not there and no one mentioned that there was another dining room,

The next morning it was dark when we assembled in the same truck to go to breakfast a full mile away. I kept looking around for Peter but by 7.20 am there was still no sign of him. The cypher offices were on the third floor of Caserta Palace, an eighteenth century building in the style of Versailles. We felt as the servants of yore must have felt, working in a comfortable, well-heated palace, living in cold, leaky hutments. The morning watch was the easy one, as messages from England did not start coming in until about 10 a.m. After that the pace quickened and built up throughout the day until 4 a.m, in the dawn watch. At 4 a.m. there was a lull, sometimes time for a nap, usually taken on the floor under the pasting table, or better still taking turns to miss the night watch.

I was allocated a machine at once, and examined it carefully. There had been developments since I was last in a central office. Each machine took a series of four drums; the order of these drums and the twenty-six settings used on each were varied each day, sometimes every six hours. There was now a greater variety of drums than there had been, each area of the war had its own special drums.

Another gadget called a slade had been introduced, which plugged into one side of the machine. This had twenty-six holes, which could be cross-connected in any combination of pairs. The combinations changed daily. All this was so complicated that at least five per cent of all messages arrived corrupt, so we could not decypher them. Usually it was a minor mistake – yesterday's slade and today's drums, for example. When we were busy these corrupt messages were piled into a basket. On the slack morning watch we would go through them to see if anyone could solve them.

I picked one of these messages and started trying it out – switching letters as well as drums. To my surprise, in five minutes I had decyphered it. I went back for another, and then another. It was my lucky day. My flight officer was delighted.

"Where did you learn all this?" she demanded. "It used to be you who made all the mistakes!"

"Perhaps that's why I'm good at finding those made by others!" I replied

"Haven't you been for coffee yet?" she asked. "It's after eleven!"

"Coffee? Where?"

"Second floor, front facing. Wander down, you'll soon see."

I wandered and the first person I saw as I walked in at the door was Peter. He stood the other side of the room by the window, the light falling on his gold-blond hair. He was flanked by his two friends and surrounded by staff officers, a number of whom I remembered from Haifa. He saw me at once and crossed the room so hurriedly the others stared after him. We stood there, staring at each other. We had not met for eighteen months, could not touch each other under all those staring eyes.

"I've just posted you a letter," he said, "what wasted effort!"

"Think how I shall enjoy reading it, when it catches up with me after the war!" I replied. His friends came over and mobbed me.

"So you've caught up with us at last!" they teased. Peter led me firmly to the coffee table. He would not see me at lunchtime because I would be late and he had to be early, but he would be in the mess that evening.

"Lucky you've arrived now. There's so much to do. Dances, operas, sightseeing, a good rest camp. We can have some fun."

"I thought there was a war on!" I commented.

"The fighting is a long way away. The Gothic line is dug in north of Florence. They'll probably stay there all winter now. By the way, what kit have you got?"

"Well, my camp equipment of course, but only one blanket. Someone liberated the other two down in East Africa. One water bottle. I have a great coat but I need blues and jerseys more than anything. I haven't needed warm clothes before."

"Go down to the officer's shop as soon as you can. You must have battle dress for the winter, and buy up several jerseys, and some warm pyjamas to wear under the battle dress. And pick up a pair of issue boots."

"Boots?" I questioned.

"Gum boots, WAAF officers, for the use of. Wait until you see our camp after a rainstorm, and you're moving on to it next month!"

I dragged myself away before we had even had time to make a firm date. I thought I had been only a few minutes, but it was now midday and the rush of work had started. I hurried to my machine and started hammering it. I was still hammering when my relief from B-Watch tapped me on the shoulder.

"Pretty awful lunch today," she commented cheerfully. "Fish and pasta, can you imagine? And tapioca pudding!"

For once I did not care what the lunch was like. I would sleep in the afternoon and then spend the evening with Peter. I would be back at the mess by 8.30 p.m and did not have to go on duty until 1.30 a.m. We could spend five whole hours together.

# Chapter 16
## Crest of a High

For eight glorious weeks I woke each morning on the crest of a high wave of happiness, with a song in my heart, unable to believe my luck. And not only because of Peter. The contrast between morale in the two theatres of war could not have been greater. In the Indian Ocean the grimness of war stretched into an unforeseeable future. The young air crew coming out were inexperienced youths doomed, within a year, to almost certain death. It was impossible to foresee a successful end to a depressing situation. Men serving in the terrible Burma Campaign considered themselves the forgotten army; all eyes, all attention, were on Allied victories in Europe.

It had not been an easy victory. Many of my friends lay in Italian graves, but we knew the fighting was nearly over. No new personnel were arriving, and everyone I met was a war-hardened veteran with a proven survival record. My own position was also much improved. Instead of the continuous responsibility for the welfare of men on active service I now worked regular hours on limited tasks with agreeable companions; my off-duty time was my own. And I did not even have to plan it. Peter arranged plenty of entertainments for us both.

On one perfect evening he took me out to dinner, borrowing a car to drive me to Naples and back. That night it took us half an hour under the dripping winter trees behind the mess to say goodnight, before I caught the transport to go on duty. Opportunities for sexual indulgence were limited in those days. Even when we managed a weekend at the RAF rest house, the best hotel in Ravallo, we were both sharing rooms with members of our own sex. Unfulfilled yearning gave a poignancy to relationships. A short break in the almost continuous wet weather enabled us to explore the famous gardens. I was happier than I had ever been.

Yet somewhere deep within me I knew something was going wrong with the relationship. I wanted to be in love with Peter, but was I really so deeply involved? Girls of my generation had been taught the bare facts of life, but had little experience of handling an affair. Some learned quickly. I did not.

Just before Christmas there was a dance at the Officers' Club in Naples, fortunately on my evening off. Peter invited me, we went down on the transport taking most of my watch to the dance, with and without escorts. After a few dances Peter left me and went off to join other men round the bar. I was determined not to be upset by a deliberate display of bad manners, and looked round the room for A-Watch. A whole group of them were sitting in one corner of the room, and I joined them, dancing several times with other men, sitting with A-Watch between times. A waiter brought us drinks and I ordered a glass of wine. In half an hour Peter came to reclaim me. I did not refer to his absence.

After a while he said, "You don't seem to mind me deserting you in strange territory."

"I'm scarcely in strange territory," I said, "with A-Watch around."

"You girls seem to get on pretty well!"

"Is that surprising? We've worked and lived together for years now."

"Women are not supposed to get on well together like that."

"Surely the war has shattered all those silly suppositions about women?"

"What about Kiwi – you didn't seem to take to her!"

"There are lots of people I find difficult, including the army catering officer at my last station, but that doesn't mean that I can't work with a wide variety of people."

I knew I was being put to the test. Weak spots were being probed out. Did I have a bad temper? Would I make a good wife for a man who would undoubtedly put career before family? He was devoted to the air force and wanted only to remain in it as long as possible.

The next test was not so easy. Returning home in the crowded transport, he tried to take the stage of petting we had reached a stage further.

**131**

For me, the man was the right one but the place, the time, and the mood were all wrong. I resisted. The slide down the wave was rapid.

Peter had some time ago taken tickets for a theatre show. A few days before, he had to go to Bari where his flight sergeant was getting married to a nursing sister; wartime weddings were arranged on the spur of the moment and he had promised to give the bride away and to propose the toast to the married couple. Now the wedding had been brought forward, he gave me the theatre tickets and asked me to take someone else. It was the middle of our long break and no one on A-Watch wanted to come. I asked an army officer, a signals type attached to the mess, a kind little man with big brown eyes who was always hanging round the WAAFs like a lost puppy longing to be petted. It was an entertaining play but a dull evening.

Two days later I went to meet Peter's plane. There was a landing strip just below Caserta and I hitched a lift down. A light plane came in, landed, slipped sideways, and burst into flames. All the alarm signals went and fire tenders raced to spray the flames. I stood there staring miserably at the debacle. My insides contracted with a terrible cramp; I knew I had started the curse although I had had it only ten days before. A black smoke arose from the pranged aircraft, carrying with it the terrible sickly sweet smell of burning human flesh.

I do not know how long I stood there, unable to move. Another plane appeared on the horizon. The pranged one, flames extinguished, was dragged off the runway towards the perimeter before the bodies were taken out. The second plane landed smoothly and taxied in to where we were standing. Peter stepped out, smiling, smart in his best blues. I stared at him dumbly. He looked at me smiling as he always did, and then his eyes glazed over, hardened. Yes, it had been a good wedding. He had drunk too much before he proposed the toast. Somehow he managed to be pompous even about a drunken party. He was not usually pompous.

He had cinema tickets for the following night. I put on my best blue uniform, my last pair of grey silk stockings and took particular care to polish shoes and buttons. Peter was very particular about appearances. He looked serious as we walked up to the garrison theatre, the private theatre for the palace and a jewel of baroque architecture. It was my favourite place of entertainment.

The night was dark and drizzling; the road full of puddles. One puddle concealed a knee-deep man hole and I walked straight into it, ruining my stockings and splashing mud all over myself. Peter pulled me out and wanted me to go back to change. I said no – we would go on to the cinema. It was dark and no one would see me.

It was as well we did for the small XVIII theatre was packed. There was a strange-looking American on my left side. It was an absorbing film, taking us well away from thoughts of war and cold and work. Suddenly I felt fingers creeping up my left thigh under my skirt. I applied a sharp blow with the side of my hand.

"Ouch!" said the stranger, withdrawing his hand hurriedly.

"What on earth is going on?" Peter leant across me protectively. "Is that man molesting you?"

"Just a little digital trouble," I joked. The man got up to leave. Peter wanted to go after him but I restrained him.

"People can't go about groping any girl they see!" he complained.

"I can assure you they do; and given the shortage of women, I'm not altogether surprised." Peter looked unhappy.

"I've had to move about a lot alone, and have learnt to look after myself," I reassured him as we came out of the cinema. I had never told him of the attack in Ismailia, one did not talk about that kind of attack in those days.

He was very quiet and I knew he was going to say something. I was still hoping he might propose. With great difficulty he said, "You know, a long relationship like ours should continue into marriage. The differences in our backgrounds would make that too difficult."

"Do differences really matter that much, Peter? You are the first generation of your family to get yourself an education, my grandfather was the first man in ours. Every family begins somewhere. And anyway, after this war social differences won't count any more."

"Yes, it might work if I felt deeply enough, but quite honestly I don't. I couldn't make that sort of commitment to you. I'm sorry."

There was nothing else to say. The wave that had lifted me so high had brought me crashing down to the depths. We waited in silence for the transport to the WAAF mess. It was exactly eight weeks since I had arrived so triumphantly. I was silent in the transport and went straight to my cubicle, thankful for privacy. Drained of all feeling, I could not sleep and could not weep. It was not even as if there was another woman. For over two years thoughts of Peter had filled much of my waking hours. Now there was nothing, nobody. And no father to console me. I felt rejected, unloved, and very sorry for myself.

If A-Watch noticed something was wrong, they were tactful enough not to say so. Usually I went late for my coffee break to coincide with Peter's; that first morning I went very early to avoid him. He'd had the same idea and was also there. We smiled at each other and turned away. There was plenty of work, and afterwards I cut lunch and set off direct from the palace on a four-hour hike along the hill tops. I had long intended to do this walk and I hoped by doing it I would be tired enough to sleep before the dawn watch.

By chance, I met the army signals officer whom I had invited to the theatre. He insisted on buying me lunch at a farmhouse, all garlic and spaghetti, and accompanied me on the rest of the walk. As we tramped along the ridge we came across ruined farm buildings and paused to look over them.

"Let's imagine how wonderfully we could do this up for ourselves, you and I!" he said.

I shuddered. "Come on, race you down, I want to catch the early transport!" Despite my dysentery, I was delighted to find I was in better fettle than he and gave him a run for his money.

Soon after, we WAAFs moved into the RAF officers' mess. No longer did we sleep in one place, eat in another, and work in a third, but there were disadvantages. Our new quarters were Nissen huts divided into two, four beds each side of the division, one watch in each hut. Nor was this lack of privacy the only shortcoming. When we moved in, the huts were under flood water so we had to use gum boots instead of bedroom slippers. Hot showers were available, a great luxury, but if you took your gum boots off it was to paddle in freezing flood water and end up with muddy feet. I tried to take a shower wearing my gum boots, but we were all laughing so much that the boots got wetter inside than I did.

It was the coldest, wettest winter in living memory, a creeping damp cold that ate into the bones. Three blankets on a camp bed were totally inadequate, and we all collected newspaper to put underneath our bedding rolls. But newspaper was needed to light the stove, and was often our only fuel to keep it going. Many a night I lay awake with the cold, wearing all my jerseys, my great coat on top of the blankets, shivering. Now we all shared one room it was not possible to read in bed. Dysentery gets worse in cold weather, and to add to my problems I became very rheumatic.

We were issued with battle dress trousers and tops, stiff rough garments but wonderfully weather proof. Only men's sizes were available, allowing plenty of room for warm layers underneath. I wore lisle stockings, a pair of men's winceyette pyjamas, and two old jerseys underneath mine. Looking like so many blue barrels, we rolled from the damp, comfortless camp to the warmth and luxury of the Palace and then rolled back again. At the Palace I always liked to use the Queen's bathroom even though it was quite a walk away; all the plaster cherubs on the ceiling wore blindfolds so they would not see the queen at her ablutions.

Soon after we moved, a vast new mess hut, cheerfully decorated and comfortably furnished, was opened. This was a great improvement, somewhere to read, write letters, play chess, in easy distance of our quarters. Inevitably, it also meant that I saw much more of Peter, and every glimpse of him reopened the wound. We would watch one another warily, unable to let each other go. Suddenly I was told it was my turn to have an extra watch off – it was the hated dawn one I could miss. This meant two nights off, time to go to Rome, which had just been opened to visitors from Caserta.

At lunchtime one mid-December day, I found a lift in a jeep heading for Rome. We followed the road which took us by Casino, and through the scenes of some of the bitterest fighting of the entire war. The destruction was terrible, each village more a ruin than was Pompei, so we could no longer make out where houses had been, and where streets. For much of the way we were driving between straight white tapes stretching through the dust and rubble – the other side of the tapes was forbidden territory not yet cleared of mines. This presented problems when I had to stop for dysentery, the more so in that a local crowd inevitably gathered from this terrible desolation to gape and to beg. On one occasion, as I got out I dropped my lunch, a packet of hard tack biscuits; in seconds a scrum of ragged dirty urchins were fighting for the biscuits.

It was dark when we drove into the outskirts of Rome, an apparently normal city which had been spared the horrors of war. All roads, all railways leading into the city had taken a strafing but the inner city was untouched. It was full of allied troops, the various hotels had been allocated for use by one or another service. Shops and businesses seemed to be flourishing. I went to the hotel taken over by the YWCA and revelled in a hot bath and a good meal. The next morning the sun came out for the first time in weeks. I had my hair done, my uniform cleaned, and then stepped out to explore. To one of my colonial upbringing, it was a revelation.

I sat for more than an hour in the square, trying to conjure up the great triumphal processions that the archway had seen. I climbed as high as was possible in the Colosseum. What had it been like to be in the middle, to see the lions coming through that door? I took an open horse carriage over the Tiber to St Peters Square, gasped at the size and proportions; climbed to the very top to gaze over the Tiber and the gardens. Inside the great building, I gazed at the Pieta and found tears streaming down my face. For the first time I understood how much women suffer when men die, for whatever cause. Yet I realized I wanted sons, wanted them more than I wanted anything else.

When I set out on the return journey it was wet again, and I had a cold bumpy ride looking out from the back of a three-ton truck at the desolate countryside through a curtain of rain. Yet I felt triumphant – I had been to Rome, and I had had a bath.

Christmas came with all its festivities. It was just a year since my father had died. I had moved heaven and earth to join Peter, and it would have been so much better if I had not done so. But I had a new understanding; others had suffered much more than I and I was determined not to mope, not even to sit around the mess hoping to be asked to join a jolly party. I took all the extra duties I could and in between concentrated on the church services. Padres were always grateful for people willing to scrub the floor of a room before they held a service in it. We were handed Christmas parcels packed by various women's associations in England, containing writing paper, soap, toothpaste, and I thought of the love and sacrifice that had gone into those parcels. I needed makeup, which was quite unobtainable, so I sent a note to Elizabeth Arden enclosing a cheque and a list. I received a huge parcel back, and inside it was enough for all A-Watch to share out. She returned the cheque, saying it was an honour to provide for us and wished us luck.

Winifred approached me; we had not seen much of each other as our hours were different and she too had her attentions engaged elsewhere. However, she had been my one confidant and we had long planned a leave in Rome together, now she had heard there was a church leadership course in Rome for one week – was I interested? Could I get leave? I went doubtfully to my flight officer. When had I last had leave? I thought back – sick leave just after my father died did not count. Not then for two years, when I went up to Haifa to see Peter. How much would I like? Would two weeks be possible? It was.

We set off again by jeep, this time we went to the RAF hotel, one of the best in Rome, and were allocated a good room. The picture galleries and museums were of course shut, but good tourists that we were, we worked through all the open-air sites. In one ancient church I asked to see the crypt, having read that it was Roman. Rather reluctantly, the friar showing us round unlocked a door and led us down some steps. There among the ancient stones were three cows – he was keeping them to provide milk for the poor of the parish. His father had a farm north of Rome but there was no transport to bring the milk in, so they had walked the cows in and hidden them in the crypt. He had to keep them locked up because with the meat shortage, who knew what might happen? All through the summer and autumn a friend had brought in the grass clippings from the public gardens, and took away the cow-pats to manure the gardens. We promised to keep his secret.

Two days later we were on the road to Assisi by staff car. One night in Assisi, a refuge seemingly untouched by war or the passing years, just time to visit the wonderful churches and stand gaping at each vista of ancient stone streets melting in winter sunshine into a golden haze. I found myself puzzling about how these ancient cities were designed. Did some artist have the vision and somehow transmute it into stone? They could surely not have grown street by street as English towns did, or they would not be so satisfyingly whole. In Florence I puzzled even harder, although the signs of war were more obtrusive. We stayed in the great hotel overlooking the dramatic black and white baptistry, stunned by the satisfying wholeness of the architecture, of the old bridge and the central square.

The war had been serious here, and the Germans had blown up all the bridges except Ponte Vecchio, where instead the houses at both ends had been demolished to delay access. The whole town was still coated in the dust of battle; many families were dragging out a miserable winter in their cellars; others had returned from mountain fastnesses to reclaim their possessions; yet more had retired to the north and were now cut off by the warring armies from returning.

We spent two days wandering about Florence, another going to Pisa, a third to Sienna. I knew little of history, nothing of art, and even less about architecture and was overwhelmed by all I saw. Every primitive painting astonished me with its beauty, with the depth of emotion conveyed by flat lines. Every lira I had was spent buying prints and photos and books, until Winifred complained at the bulk of my luggage

It was difficult to spend as much time as we wished on sightseeing for there were no servicewomen north of Rome and everywhere we went, parties were organized for us. One young flying officer, Taffie, took us to his mess high above Florence and ran us round in an Italian sports car. He had an impressive knowledge of architecture and was a kind and thoughtful guide, but I took so little interest in him that a fortnight later I did not even remember his name.

We returned to Rome in the back of an open truck, blue with cold, alternatively showered by dust and soaked by rain. Our course was in a small hotel right in the centre. As we were the only women we had been allocated the best room with a splendid marble bathroom attached.

"Just look at this," I crowed, locking Winifred out to indulge my usual complaint. I pulled the plug and a rush of water swept the entire contents across the marble floor. There was no hot water and no cold either except spasmodically for the loo, whose drainage frequently blocked.

Meals were served in a restaurant some distance away, and on the way back from supper on our first day we passed a hotel set aside for senior army officers. Since our hotel had such terrible plumbing, we had decided to try our luck in obtaining a bath and washing our hair in some other hostelry, and this looked just the job. We walked into this posh hotel and asked at the desk if there was a bathroom we could use.

"No," said the clerk.

"Yes," said a major standing at the desk, "my friend and I have a suite and I know he won't mind. You are welcome to use it."

He took us upstairs to rooms even more luxurious than ours, and we were shown through living room and bedroom to the bathroom. We went in together, locked the door, and stripped for a bath and hair-washing session, deciding we might also wash our underclothes. We were both at our wettest when the door handle waggled. We turned off the taps to hear the voices outside.

"What have you locked the door for?" We did not answer. "Open it at once, you naughty girls!"

No answer. Weight was applied to the door, and the lock looked as if it might loosen. I rushed to put by back against it, wedging my legs against the bath. The lock held. Winifred finished her shower quickly and then took my place while I dried. We threw on our clothes, to an increasingly angry commentary from outside. Neither of us had been able to rinse our hair properly, and dirty soapy water was trickling down our collars. We looked hardly better than when we came in as we buttoned ourselves into overcoats and crammed caps on our heads. We had intended to accept a drink if it was offered, but now we would dash through the bedroom towards the sitting room, saying thank you as we went.

The two majors had planned their strategy carefully: the short fat one was to take his pick in the bedroom, releasing the other one of us into the sitting room to the tall thin major who had brought us up. Fortunately the fat one was so befuddled with drink that we pushed past him easily, but when we reached the outer door, it was locked. The key had been taken out.

"What sort of thank you is that?" The tall thin major sat back in his chair and licked his lips.

"No thank you at all, if you ask me," said the fat one, trundling unsteadily after us.

"Are you girls going to be in Rome long?" the first major asked, determined to appear urbane.

"Yes, a week, on the church leadership course!" I said.

"The what?"

"The church leadership course." The door opened as if by magic. We were released into the traffic-less streets of Rome, leaving two angry, frustrated army officers behind us.

The course was my first experience of adult education. I had applied for it out of curiosity, with no real idea what it might contain, because it would give me a whole week in Rome. To my surprise, the subject matter proved completely absorbing. I had inherited my father's interest in ancient history, and this was the first time that I had heard the Bible presented as a history of God's revelation to man; the Roman Empire as the medium through which the New Testament was transmitted to the world, the Roman church as the organization which had preserved it, the Protestants as the ones who had re-interpreted the message.

Best of all were the hours we spent wandering around Rome with skilled guides, using the monuments and treasures of Rome as exclamation marks to our studies. At last I began to understand why the primitive school of painting had made such an impression on me. I learned why the architecture lifted the mind and filled the spirit. The Pieta in St Peters still moved me in depths I had not known existed, and I found the other famous pieta in the crypt of St John Lateran almost more satisfying. My own disappointments and grief were pushed to the back of my mind. A great peace, a completeness filled my spirit. From that moment on I began to see shortcomings in the up-tightness, the self-righteousness, of the Protestant ethic. One day I too would return to the fount of Western Christianity, to the shelter of the Catholic Church.

In the evenings we were encouraged to discuss moral problems – problems which were in those days difficult to put into words. It worried me greatly that I was so actively engaged helping to kill my Austrian cousins. Was I really justified in so doing? Unfortunately yes, most of our choices were between two evils and letting Hitler win the war would be the greater evil. After the war my contacts must be used for forgiveness, and as a channel of peace.

Another personal problem was that all of us women were constantly propositioned by men desperate for sex at any price. Were we right to deny them, even when that day might be their last? Did we price our virginity too high? Certainly we were right to hold out, we could not oblige them all, and the fact that we kept high standards was in itself cheering to men whose own women were far away. The difficulties of marriages long separated by war were thrashed out. It was a shock to realize how ignorant I was, how little I had experienced.

It was the first time in five years that I took time to stand back and look at myself and the world I lived in. During those five years I had grown up. There was time to make decisions and I made them. Almost all women of my generation regarded marriage both as a preferred option and as a full-time occupation. You chose career or marriage, at the best a career until marriage came along. It was time to make plans for the future.

The course served to convince me that I must resume my studies, no question of getting married or settling down until I had several years' reading behind me. Then if marriage offered, I would insist on a career as well. I would never fall in love easily again, but I could leave the world a better, happier place. What an earnest little prig I must have been.

# Chapter 17
## Roll on that Boat

When I returned to Caserta in the third week of January, the weather had changed, the sun was shining. A-Watch, as always, gave me a warm welcome.

"That dishy wing-co of yours was asking after you," said one. "He seemed quite anxious that you had disappeared. Didn't you tell him where you were going?"

"You are a dark horse, June," said another, "a super flying type with Prune's moustaches came asking after you, saying he must find you; he said he'd met you in Florence and loved you madly." Flying Officer Prune was the creation of a well-known cartoonist, a favourite character from our airforce manuals, the man who always did everything wrong.

"Glad someone does," I murmured. "How's the work?"

"Terrible; doubled since the weather improved. All sorts of things happening. Special Cyphers have doubled – I think you're up for that!"

MAAF HQ was a combined headquarters in that it housed all the Allied Air Forces. The RAF cypher office also dealt with cyphers for the British Government and with material recyphered from German cyphers broken at Betchley Park. A special cypher office had been set up to handle only this top secret material, mostly Churchill's communications to Commanders in Chief and discussions about future operations. Early in 1945 papers to set up the Yalta conference were coming in, and while the conference was on we did all the signals, flown in to us from Yalta so we could encypher and decypher them.

It was an exciting place to work. There was only room for two of us in the tiny, windowless room. We had to work fast and accurately. Many messages were so secret that only two people saw them, the WAAF who worked on them and the man to whom they were addressed. This meant that as soon as we had decyphered the address, we had to phone the officer concerned, and arrange to deliver the message to him in person when we had completed it. Aides, personal secretaries and others senior to us in rank and years, were on occasion quite annoyed when we refused to hand the message over to them; we had always to insist on giving it to the great man himself. We had also to be band-box smart as we might have to break in on some important conference. Battle dress (i.e. nice warm trousers!) could only be worn on night watch.

If the message arrived in the small hours of the night, we sent a messenger to find the officer wherever he might be, and to find out where to deliver it. Some senior officers preferred to come to the cypher office and write out their replies at once; others preferred to find message and decypherer waiting in their offices, and yet others wanted the message taken down to their tents. When you are a very junior officer, do you salute the general if he is sitting on the edge of a camp bed in a bright red dressing gown, blinking in the light of a hurricane lamp, stroking a very unshaven chin with one hand as he fumbles a pencil across a signals pad with the other?

Although I only worked in this office when there was a flap on, I gleaned all kinds of information: the Russian insistence that the Allies did not advance too far east, the political realities behind the resistance movements in Yugoslavia and Greece, the need to move men and materials to Burma, the bits of the horrifying jigsaw puzzle slotting into place. When I first saw that under the terms of the Yalta Conference, Russia was to seize all Austrian assets developed by the Germans, my mind seethed. The oil discovered only in 1938 would be lost. What would poor Austria do? But so ingrained was the habit of secrecy that I never discussed it.

A circular came round asking if anyone had any pre-war knowledge of Northern Italy or of the Tyrol to interpret the reconnaissance photos coming in prior to our advance over the Brenner. I filled in the form, and some days later I found myself in the reconnaissance room, where photos of the Lower Inn Valley were put on a screen. Jenbach, five miles from Matzen, was easy to recognize, and the railway workshop lay in ruins; I did not know the caves in the mountain above Jenbach. Yes, I had walked past there and never seen them. Much later I learnt that parts for the V1 and V2 bombs were manufactured in those caves by slave workers from Eastern Europe. In 1945 the caves were filled in and abandoned, with the workers inside.

We moved a few miles further east, to the next railway bridge across the River Inn – or rather, the next empty space where a beautiful wooden bridge had once stood. Yes, that was the copper works. I gulped, horrified at the destruction.

"What is this tower?" The pointer continued relentlessly.

"Schloss Matzen, my grandmother's castle!"

"Are you sure?"

"Yes, absolutely sure. I spent many of my school holidays there."

Very hesitantly someone said, "We've heard it's occupied by Nazi sympathisers!"

"Possibly, we haven't heard what has happened to it."

"They claim to be relations of the owner."

"Very possibly; my grandfather's sisters married Austrians and big families are often divided."

"What is in the tower? Do you think ack ack guns could be hidden in there?"

I remembered running up the steep staircases from one rough round room to the next, all of them dark and empty. The top room had more light, and wonderful views up and down the valley from its little loopholes. In the centre of the room stood a huge post from which rough-hewn beams radiated like spokes, and on these spokes rested the structure which supported the conical roof. We children would scramble up the wall, balance-walk across one of the spokes to the centre post, to which we had fastened a ladder to take us to another layer of spokes high in the roof cone. On these we had laid a floor of rough boards, and this perch had become our hideout, our secret play area, our retreat on wet afternoons, the place to keep old toys, snaffled biscuits and forbidden books.

"Most unlikely. You see the roof comes low down and the loopholes are small, so unless they took the roof off, ack ack guns would be useless, they couldn't swing round. Also the place is a protected building and if the present occupants are family they wouldn't put Matzen at risk from bombing. Guns would be more useful here."

I took the pointer to a summer house standing on a knoll about fifty metres from Matzen, another favourite play area but not nearly so romantic as the tower. The questioning rod moved on.

"What is this building on top of this hill?"

"A war memorial chapel for the 1914-18 War."

"Would guns be placed there?"

"Possibly, but from the chapel their view might be limited. Lower down ancient mine shafts go into the hill horizontally, and would provide better cover. That? An ancient pilgrimage chapel, not often used. Those are only hay alms."

The rod moved east again. The sprawling village seemed to lie in ruins. I wondered what had happened to our friends, to priest, doctor, schoolmaster, butcher, baker, grocer, postmaster, tailor, shoemaker, and a host of others, all the people we knew and on whom we had depended. In the Seychelles it had been easy to believe the only good German was a dead one; now, when I saw the devastation we had wrought, I was no longer sure. Those villagers were good people, hard-working, kindly, honest, steeped deep in their old traditions. What had happened to them? Who was dead and who survived?

Life was not all hard work. There was an enthralling visit to Pompei – in those days women were not allowed to see the graffiti so we stood outside while the men went in. Then there was Vesuvius, which had recently erupted and was still very hot underfoot. I made the mistake of refusing to be parted from my greatcoat, worn over battle dress and warm pyjamas, and was so weighed down that I rumbled and puffed almost as energetically as the volcano beneath us. It was a struggle to get to the top and peer down through the hot, all-enveloping vapours, so dense that they prevented any view, into the crater or out to sea.

Once, when my day off happened to be Sunday, Winifred and I went to the RAF rest hotel at Rapallo. When we walked into the dining room there was a party of senior RAF officers, including Peter and his two friends. Everyone assumed Peter and I had arranged this meeting; his neighbour got up with his plate and I was pushed into his chair. Winifred caught my eye and grinned. I tried to look cheerful.

"It's no good, we can't get away from each other!" Peter said quietly.

How I wished it were true. My insides had been gripped with cramp all day and I could eat nothing.

"Still the same trouble?" Peter asked.

"Yes," I replied.

"You must see the doc!"

"All very well to say. He'll only say I'm emotionally upset."

Peter looked at me sideways to see if I was getting at him. "Has he said that?" he asked.

"Haven't been to a doc since I left Nairobi; he was sympathetic, but that's what they said at TME."

"That's more than a year ago now," said Peter.

"Yes, it seems even longer." To my horror I felt tears coming. I turned hastily to my other neighbour and struck up a conversation. Soon after I returned to Caserta, the MO sent for me; Peter had obviously been at work. He examined me thoroughly, said he thought I might have a grumbling appendix or any one of several tropical illnesses, and that I should return to England on the next boat.

"That suits me all right," I said. Arrangements went ahead quickly.

The main battle of the Atlantic was over, but there were a number of German submarines working off the coast of Portugal which were still operating and still managed a number of kills. In order to keep move-ments of troops secret, travellers were assembled in transit camps a few days before a boat was due to sail. Quite soon I was told when to report, and coincidentally Taffy appeared on the scene, flying in one Sunday morning, surprised to find me on watch. Over lunch in the mess he tried to persuade me up to Florence again. At first I refused, but his offer to fetch me and bring me back in a reconnaissance plane was irresistible. Two days before I had to report to the transit camp, Taffy whisked me up to Florence, put me up in his mess, drove me around to explore the city. He was still flying reconnaissance flights over Austria.

"Could you get me some pictures of Matzen, my grandparents' home, Taffy?" I asked.

"Piece of cake," he replied, "going that way tomorrow. Won't be ready before you sail, but I'll send them back. You will go and visit my mum, won't you? I've told her about you!"

"What about me? Taffy, I've told you I'm more interested in going to university than in settling down. I'm not taking you seriously."

"Yes, I know all that, but do go and see Mum, I know she'll love to have news of me!"

"All right, Taffy, I'll go mum-visiting; I'm doing it for several other mums as well." I did not tell him the others were mums of my WAAF friends. From Taffy's viewpoint it was a good thing I was leaving; he would soon find someone else and forget me. Meanwhile his admiration was balm to my battered ego. I liked the way he made no physical demands of me, not even holding my hand, and I took it as a matter of course that he should want to write to me.

To my joy, Winifred was leaving on the same boat. The embarkation camp was luxuriously accommodated in a series of villas overlooking Naples Harbour, now sparkling in early April sunshine. Once again our room had a grand marble bathroom; this one was divorced from any water supply. We decided to remain dirty rather than go out looking for a bathroom. Security was no longer enforced as strictly as it had been, and we were allowed out of camp to go sightseeing. The ruined town of Heraculaneum proved even more touching in its abandonment than was Pompei. Bodies had been left as they had been found: the woman and child, the pet dog, who did not quite make an escape, had been petrified for ever by the lava flowing from Vesuvius two thousand years previously. The bygone splendours of ancient villas contrasted oddly with the squalor of modern Naples.

Late one evening in early April we folded up our camp beds and wash basins, rolled them in our bedding rolls, shouldered our kit bags, picked up our suitcases, and in the early darkness marched on board. The ubiquitous greeting and letter ending – Roll On That Boat – had happened, at last, to us.

Just before we sailed, an urgent letter was delivered to me. It was from Taffy, a fulsome declaration of his love. There was nothing I could do; locked in the secrecy of wartime travel, I had to remain out of all contact with the world until we arrived in Blighty. We had met precisely three times and I was emotionally numb. I put the letter out of my mind, but it would be intriguing to meet his mum.

# Chapter 18
## Bomb-blighted Britain

In peacetime the sea journey from Naples to Britain took a week; now we had no idea how long it would take. We crossed to Gibraltar and waited for the convoy to assemble. The uncertainty of life exacerbated everyday discomforts of too many people, too little space, and a tiny fresh water ration. Six women were crammed into a cabin intended for three: three ENSA girls, three WAAF officers. Our wash basin had water in the tap for twenty minutes twice a day; six of us had to wash ourselves, our teeth, our hair and, hopefully, our clothing.

The troops were far less comfortable than ourselves, packed into the holds, layer on layer of them. On each level huge tables had been set up, on these the men ate meals, wrote letters, read books, played games. At night some of them slept on the tables, others slung hammocks above them. Plates, mugs, and washing up bowls were kept under the tables.

Meals in the officers' dining room were on a three-shift system. The decks were too crowded for the usual games or exercise. Three times a day we assembled for lifeboat drill. We had to wear life-jackets all the time, and were supposed to sleep in them. The 'Mae Wests', as they were called, were bright yellow and gave everyone that well-padded look up front. On the left shoulder was fastened a torch which – at the touch of a button – flashed a red light. Inevitably it was nicknamed a 'Piccadilly'. Round our necks dangled police whistles, known as coppers. In addition, we had to carry bags packed with emergency supplies around with us. From dusk to dawn we were all battened down in our quarters; no movement on deck was allowed.

Despite all the discomforts, there was an all-pervading atmosphere of joy and good nature such as I have rarely experienced. We were the lucky ones, the ones returning home. Except for the time OC troops got into our cabin in the early hours (we were not allowed to shut doors in case they jammed in an attack) and from my upper bunk I kicked him in his face, I did not hear a single angry word during the entire interminable three weeks.

In the dark of a moonless night we slipped through the Straits of Gibraltar and the sea roughened. Although it was so near the end of the war, submarines were still being sent out from Germany. They lurked along the coasts of Portugal and Spain, and in the one month of February 1945, the Germans deployed forty new and faster U boats in British coastal waters. To avoid them we sailed due west every day for nearly a week, until we thought, surely America must hove into view tomorrow.

At last the tomorrow arrived when the sun woke us, pouring into our starboard porthole.

"Looks like we've turned!" said Winifred, from the middle bunk.

"So we have!" I leant down from the top one and tried to peer out of the porthole.

"How do you know?" asked the ENSA girls.

"Black magic!" we replied in one voice.

The convoy grew steadily; we never knew where the extra ships had come from, but by now there were at least thirty vessels of all shapes and sizes sailing in a diamond formation, keeping exactly in position, our escorting destroyers spread out round the points of the diamond, nudging us along like sheepdogs. It was an impressive display of discipline and seamanship, particularly when the whole convoy wheeled around to change directions. The outer boats had obviously to move faster than those inside the turn, and it was done with perfect precision. Such a huge diamond of a convoy was sure to invite trouble when we reached the narrow waters round Britain. It did.

We sighted the southern tip of Ireland, swung round to the north and were in the Irish Channel. We all stood at the rail for hours in a cold drizzle, watching for our first sight of the country we had fought for, but were hurried below decks earlier than usual, before the lump on the horizon could become a lump in our throats.

The sea grew choppier and the tannoy called its relentless instructions, more frenzied than at any time during the voyage. No one was to undress, even to wash, nor to take off his life-jacket, nor be parted from his emergency bag. Supper – soup, bread, an apple – was served to all three sittings at once, standing up in the dining saloon. As we left, we were handed a packet of emergency rations to pack in our bags. That night we lay like stranded whales in the darkness of our bunks, wedged into the narrow, coffin-like space by the thickness of coats and life jackets.

I imagined the long night watch in cypher offices and operations rooms, where plotters were marking our course and the enemy's in an endeavour to keep us safe. The hours crept past slowly. In the small hours of the morning the slap of waves and vibrations of the pitching ship were interrupted by a loud explosion. Everything in the cabin shook and rattled. We all lay silent, cold at heart, clutching our emergency bags like teddy bears, waiting for another explosion, for the siren, for something that would tell us what had happened. The ship remained in silence. Depth charges thudded near us, then gradually further away. There were no announcements.

Next morning we struggled out of our bunks onto the deck, no need to waste time getting dressed, and learnt that the boat between us and the destroyer had been torpedoed and had sunk rapidly. Two or three lifeboats had been picked up, sixty survivors from many hundreds. That people should die on the last stretch of the journey home seemed more poignant, more pointless than other losses had been.

The British coast lay grey and desolate to starboard. At Glasgow we had to wait our turn to dock. Nobody grumbled, not after last night. We'd survived. The grimness of grey, wartorn Glasgow cut to the heart – sadder than the sunlit poverty of southern Italy. We were taken off by lighter, climbing down narrow ladders into the rocking boat. In groups of fifty or sixty, shouldering our kit bags, we marched along the dock to a waiting train which took us into Glasgow Central Station. Women in WVS uniform handed out mugs of tea; scouts and guides handed us oranges which we felt we had to accept although they needed them more than we did. The route was lined by cheering Cubs and Brownies waving flags.

We three WAAFs went to the main station hotel, washed in freely flowing hot water, and sat down to our first civilized dinner. It was sparse by pre-war standards, but seemed luxurious to us. This was not an occasion for economy. We ordered generously, drinking brandy before the meal and wine with it. When we came to pay, we were told our bill had been paid for us; Scotsmen the other side of the room would not hear of the 'heroic lassies' buying their own meal. We went to thank them, and they carried our kit bags to the night train and waved us God speed.

Around seven on a sunny spring morning towards the end of April, Winifred and I parked our luggage at Euston Station and set out for my uncle's address in Great Russell Street. As we came on to the Euston road, two very smart senior squadron officers went by. I had my kit bag in my right hand and was not quick about saluting. The squadron officer turned on me savagely.

"What unit are you from?"

"MAAF HQ, Ma'am!"

"And where is that?"

"Mediterranean Allied Air Forces, Ma'am, just east of Naples."

"You can't be from Italy. You haven't got an Italy star up!"

"Italy star, ma'am?"

"The ribbon you get for serving in Italy." Her voice was even more irritable; she looked at me as if I were an imbecile.

"No, Ma'am, they didn't reach us out there!"

"And why are you wearing such a ridiculous hat? Where is your uniform cap?" I looked at Winifred helplessly.

"Lost two years ago in the desert, Ma'am!" No need to say in a foolish sailing accident.

"Well, why didn't you replace it?"

"There weren't any women's caps where we were, Ma'am.!"

"And why are you wearing battle dress in London? It looks a terrible mess!"

"Indeed, Ma'am, I haven't taken it off for nearly a week!"

"Not taken it off for a week! What do you mean?"

"It's like that on a troopship, Ma'am."

I looked over my shoulder conspiratorially. We were not supposed to reveal our recent arrival, shipping movements were top-secret and we had been briefed to keep silent for a week, but there was no way out.

"Well, you will report to me correctly dressed later today, at AHQ. And now I want your name and your English unit." She stressed the English, and it was hard to persuade her.

Fifteen minutes later we were ringing the bell outside my uncle's flat in the worst part of blitzed Bloomsbury. Everything was enveloped in a coating of grey sludge. His head emerged through a window two storeys up.

"Well done! Well done, young women! Any trouble?" His voice was that of a naval officer trained in the days before tannoys.

He threw down a key. We retrieved it and let ourselves in before replying, still two floors away: "A bit, two nights ago. Irish channel, one hit. I think your chaps got it. About sixty survivors."

"Yes, I thought that might be you! Glad you weren't on the target! Reporting to Kingsway today?" He gave me an enormous hug.

"Yes, I'm on a disciplinary charge already, wrong dress!" I told him of the WAAF officer.

"Silly bitch!" he commented.

"I must say I do feel welded into my clothes. Haven't taken them off for nearly a week!" I had by now glimpsed myself in the hall mirror and seen how dishevelled I looked.

"Well, get into the bathroom, the two of you, and then I'll give you a lift to AHQ. We can stop to buy new caps at Grieves en route." He limped off to put on his admiral's uniform.

"You'll stay with us of course?" my aunt asked as we emerged shades cleaner from the bathroom. She handed me a huge pile of letters, all of them from Taffy, none from my mother as I could not tell her I was moving. My aunt had cooked their combined egg ration for a week for our breakfasts, one boiled egg each. Now we sat polishing the buttons of our clean uniforms, blackened by sea air.

"Winifred is going north and has asked me to go with her. You haven't room!" I protested. They had one small bedroom, a sitting room in which they had to eat as the kitchen was too small, and a windowless dressing room. There was nothing impressive about an admiral's lodgings in wartime London.

"There's always room for you, you can bed down in the sitting room," my aunt replied. "Your Great Aunt Maud died two days ago and the funeral is tomorrow; it will be a chance to meet all the family. Also you must visit your grandmother. Go up north later."

She was in her mid-fifties but still looked as beautiful as she had in Cairo, tall and erect, blue-eyed and golden-haired. Only the smooth face was now strained and showing signs of age, there was a tenseness about her mouth, in her voice. She looked desperately tired. Her three men had been in constant action throughout a long war; even now her two sons were in the Far East, and the admiral was waiting to go to Germany to take over Kiel.

The admiral's car, flag flying to signify 'admiral on board', drove us down to Grieves where the old man insisted on helping us choose uniform caps. His presence certainly made for instant and hilarious service, as he tried on each cap himself.

A few minutes later we disembarked outside AHQ with a great deal of saluting and counter-saluting going on. It was with trepidation that I entered the building, wondering what the outcome of the disciplinary charge would be, although I was more afraid of myself than of others. I had hardly slept for two nights, had eaten and drunk too much the night before, and knew how uncertain my temper was.

The first part of the visit was a routine reception, and a generous one. We were issued with the various necessities for life in England: ration book, clothing coupons, petrol coupons, four weeks' leave, rail travel vouchers, an advance of pay due to us. Our old pay books were taken from us and we were formally thanked for our service.

The squadron officer who had seen me that morning was not welcoming, but she had modified both voice and manner. She kept me standing to attention and came round from her desk to inspect me.

"When did you last have your hair cut?"

"Three months ago, in Rome, Ma'am."

"Did you have a very bad journey?" The voice was kinder now.

"No, it was good really, except for the shortage of water and the overcrowding. On the last night, one of the convoy was hit. It seemed so terrible, in sight of home."

"I'm sorry," she said, and I wondered what she was sorry about, her earlier outburst, or the ship going down. War was such a mix-up between triviality and tragedy. "Would you like to go on an Admin course for officers, three weeks in Stratford-on-Avon?"

"Very much," I replied. I noticed a shadowy figure through an open door communicating with the next office.

As I left, a WAAF orderly came after me and led me back into this office through a different entrance. The connecting door was now shut. The group officer sitting behind the desk (much senior to the squadron officer next door) stood up to greet me, made me sit down, and ordered coffee. She kept me talking for well over an hour, finding out all she could about service in Italy, about the journey home, about me, concerned that I was tired and strained.

"I think you need somewhere where you can go and just sleep and sleep," she said at last. I nodded, feeling tears coming at such kindness. "Mind you get in touch if you need any help," she said as I left. I felt relieved to have a friend in a high place, oblivious to the fact that in my weariness I had taken no note of her name. To this day I do not know who she was.

The next day there was the family funeral. Aunt Maud was the last survivor of my grandmother's unmarried sisters, who had been 'the aunts' to over thirty nephews and nieces of my mother's generation, and remained `the aunts' for ours. Maiden aunts were wonderful in times of domestic emergency. My sisters and I had spent many holidays with them, when our parents were abroad. Throughout the war Aunt Maud had continued to serve the family by caring for my grandmother – cut off from her Austrian home as she was. The clan of relatives who gathered for the funeral down in Surrey were genuinely grieving. All the younger ones were in uniform, and as I followed Tom into the tiny country church I heard the question:

"Who's the WAAF with the admiral?"

"Olga's youngest from Kenya!"

As we went out for the internment, there was a sort of gasp – Maud had been a very big woman, the coffin was a tiny box the size of a briefcase. We had not realized that she had been cremated first in order to find room in the family grave. Tea was served at the home of old playmates from my grandmother's childhood – old spinster ladies who had lived on in their family home. Spring had touched the garden generously, the sun was shining, the tea was delicious, cousins whom I had not met since the schoolroom crowded round me to exchange news. Invitations showered on me, and were gladly accepted. It was good to be part of a large family.

More distressing was visiting my grandmother in a nursing home in the suburbs of London. I remembered so vividly finding her on her bedroom floor six years earlier. Since then I had experienced what seemed like aeons of travel and adventure, sorrow and happiness, which had changed me from inky school girl to competent WAAF officer. All that time she had lain between four walls, her lively mind imprisoned in a helpless body, her speech limited to making approving or disapproving sounds, her movement to waving her left hand around.

"She won't know who you are, you mustn't mind! She's going blind, and nearly deaf," my uncle warned me. I wondered how to greet her, would 'Hallo Granny' be too much of a shock? I took off my cap as I went into her room. She smiled at me, clucking with excitement, and as I hugged her she pointed to a photo of my father, shaking her head sadly; next she pointed to a picture of my sister Ronny with her baby and clapped her good hand against the paralysed arm. In thirty seconds she had placed me precisely, and commented on recent events in my family life. Next she picked up a photo of my mother and looked beseechingly at me.

"Mother is well, Granny," I said, and walked to the window to hide tears. There was a cherry tree in full flower outside the window. "You see that tree, Granny, with its beautiful white blossom? When it comes into fruit the war will be over and then Mother will come to see you!" She reached for her spectacles and put them on with her left hand, looked at the tree, and nodded at me. She patted the bed for me to sit near her, patted my uniform to show approval.

I took up her photos one by one and told her the news about each person; and then about all those I had met the day before, but I did not mention the funeral. Hours later I was still there, holding her hand while she slept.

My family was nothing if not varied. My father's sister was a nun in an Anglican convent at Ascot. I was invited to stay. Heads had to be covered all the time. However, when they saw how ridiculous a veil looked with a uniform, and had agreed that my cap should not be worn indoors, an exception was made. I went bare-headed. The guest-rooms in the convent were extremely comfortable, and the food good. My aunt was delighted to see me, spoke to me for hours about my father, and led me round the convent's old ladies' home and infant school as if I were a prize exhibit. She had the same turn of mind as my father and myself. I had come for one night but stayed for three. In that time we became fast friends.

Taffy continued to write, and I set out to visit his mother. She was a small woman, much younger than my mother or aunt, impeccably turned out, living a privileged life in a large house in Hampshire. Her husband was still away in the war. The visit was an unnerving experience. Taffy had not hidden his feelings about me, and I was welcomed as a future daughter-in-law. The house was beautifully furnished and every time I admired anything she would look at me and say, "All this will be Taffy's one day."

Taffy's younger sisters did not seem to mind, but I was embarrassed. There was no petrol to take me anywhere, and over the silver cleaning that seemed to be so much on his mother's mind, I kept stressing that I was on my way to Oxford and had no intention of settling down, while she kept apologizing for all the things wrong with the house, and then – when the daughters were not there – suddenly surprised me with a frank discussion of her own sex life. Had she fathomed my ignorance? Was she trying to draw me out? Did she need a confidant? Did she think I needed information?

This visit served to bring home to me how rough my manners had become. I was by now good at mess life, able to live amicably at close quarters with complete strangers from all walks of life, but I was entirely undomesticated. I had difficulty in remembering that cups had saucers, that a clean plate was used for every course, that meals had to be attended punctually and served ritualistically. Nor was I any use in a kitchen.

Oxford was welcoming. I was the first returning WAAF to visit Lady Margaret Hall and was entertained regally at high table, which gave me a wonderful view of the undergraduates. I could not see one well-dressed, pretty girl among them; clothes were rationed and the girls were wearing a mixture of outgrown school uniforms and unsuitable hand-me-downs; they had rolls of puppy fat from a diet of carbohydrates; hair seemed a bedraggled mess. Did I want to join them, to go back to school? I was delighted to hear that Jo Moore from Kenya was coming up. There would be one familiar face, and Jo's style of dressing should go down big.

At high table the food was bad but the conversation excellent. I had been seated near three dons of the schools I was considering, and each in turn gave me a summary of her subject. For years I had been wavering between english and history, with an occasional meditation on such subjects as mathematics or law. The lack of any sixth form education cut out both the latter. Towards the end of the meal, Mrs Kneale, the tutor in philosophy, asked me, "Which newspaper do you read?"

"The Times, when I can get it."

She started discussing current issues; I recognized recent leading articles and responded accordingly. She smiled.

"I think it's politics, philosophy, and economics for you!" I had not heard of this course before, and when I did, I agreed at once.

"There's an entrance exam in June. If you can reach scholarship standard we could ask for you to be released to come up this year!"

It sounded too good to be true, and it was. After the exam I had a kind letter telling me I came up to entrance standard, not scholarship. I should try again in the autumn for the following year.

Aunt Maud's house, Browns, in Robertsbridge, had to be sold, and the contents auctioned. The entire family assembled at the sale. Bidding was highest for the silly things: the old family gong, the weighing machine that had been in the upstairs bathroom. I was delighted when the former went to my godmother, and even more delighted when forty years later it came to me. At the sale I could not bid for anything, I had nowhere to put it.

While I was still on leave, Germany at last capitulated. My two cousins and my brother-in-law were all in the Far East, so the family did not feel ready to rejoice, yet to be in London for VE Day was a reason for rejoicing in itself. Wheel traffic seemed to disappear and the streets were jam-packed with happy, laughing, rejoicing crowds. Whole families strung together hand in hand wove their way through the hordes. From Piccadilly Circus to Trafalgar Square, all down Whitehall, people thronged so thickly that movement was almost impossible. My new cap was pulled from my head as often as I put it on, usually by exuberant American sailors, who demanded a kiss to give it back again. At all costs, I was going to keep that cap.

Civilians were shabbily dressed, the women mostly in headscarves, hair stringy, lined faces innocent of makeup. The young were all in uniform, and looked in contrast smart and well-fed. All were united in joy and happiness, yet it was easy to pick out the bereaved, the sad eyes above the smiling mouths. Outside Buckingham Palace the crowds thronged suffocatingly, calling for Winston Churchill, for the King, for the princesses, and then for Winston again. It was a powerful display of mass emotion rarely experienced in Britain. It was a memorable day, one of the most important in all our lives. Britain had been blighted, now it was blessed.

# Chapter 19
## RAF Hospital Wendover

After Victory in Europe, each one of us had to take an important decision. Did we volunteer for a tour of duty in the Far East, or did we press for an early release in Britain? For me the decision rested upon health.

Meanwhile my mother had arrived back, wangling an air passage despite the dozens of people wanting to return to England. I first knew of her arrival when I walked into my grandmother's room and found her kneeling at her mother's bedside to have her hair combed. My grandmother always greeted Olga's wayward hair with a comb at the ready. They were both weeping with emotion.

"What are you going to do next?" she asked.

"I don't know if I'll get out this round," I said, "there's still a war on in the Far East."

Release from the RAF was on a complicated system of points – according to age and length of service. I was already serving with Bomber Command at Stanmore when my papers from Italy caught up with me and with them the report that I must have a medical check-up. The doctor, very young and keen, discovered that I was five years younger than the age entered on my papers and insisted on amending them. This meant I would have to serve longer. It also convinced him I was in perfect health, feigning illness to get an early release. I was sure I had some kind of tropical bug; he took one blood test, pronounced me healthy but tired, and offered me a week's sick leave. I declined. After four weeks' demob leave I did not need any more. I had no idea of the tests which should have been done on me, and unfortunately neither had he. He recommended I started to smoke, to calm my nerves.

To my mother I said how sorry I was to be going on a course just when she arrived, that in August I would be due for leave and I hoped I would be able to tell her when I was likely to get out of the service, and yes, I still wanted to go to Oxford, had taken the first steps to achieving this, and that a grateful government was going to pay for me to do so.

Before I left Stanmore, I had to pay my mess bill. It was a tiny amount but I had had no pay since I first arrived in England because my new pay book had not arrived. I had now been back six weeks, and had spent all my money. I went to the pay officer requesting an advance on the six weeks of pay owing to me, but was told nothing could happen until the new pay book arrived.

"I can't pay my mess bill!" I said.

"Mess bills have to be paid!" he said firmly. "Why don't you borrow from your father?"

"That would be awkward, sir. St. Peter might not let me in! I've been helping my mother, rather than the other way round." I still found it difficult to speak of my father's death.

He smirked. "There's always some way a pretty girl like you can borrow a bit of money!"

I walked out of his office as rudely as I could, and told our mess secretary that I could not pay my bill. She hated having to report me to the officer commanding, although I said, "Please do, it's the only way I shall get any money!"

The interview took place with his deputy that afternoon. He was so annoyed that a girl should have been left without pay for six weeks that I did not dare tell him about the accountant officer's remark, as I had intended. Money arrived in half an hour, the bill was paid, and I was on my way.

The course was for three weeks in June, at Stratford on Avon. I was billeted in the hotel just opposite the theatre, and managed to obtain tickets for a dozen performances. For me it was a kind of theatre festival, an education in Shakespeare. There was a run of the historical plays, and I started reading English history avidly. The countryside was at its best in early June, and evenings could be spent on the river. For the first time in my working life, I was working normal office hours.

The course itself was useful but too late for me. It explained all kinds of service procedures I had been puzzling over for years. I liked the method of teaching, which was done by making us act out situations we might find difficult – how an interview should, and should not, be conducted, how a junior should be told off, how a request should be refused, how important the tone of voice was. I did not excel at the drilling and on one occasion lost my platoon marching into the morning mist, not knowing how to recall them. Feeling much more confident as well as more educated, I returned to London and called in on my aunt.

"You don't look any better," she said.

"The RAF seem to think I'm all right."

"The trouble is that I don't know any suitable specialists in London. As a doctor's daughter, I used to know them all."

"There's always Mr. Parsons Smith. Do you remember, I went to him when I had heart problems as a child."

She rang him up at once. He had last seen me in 1938. Now he looked at me with approval, perhaps because his son, also a doctor, was a group captain in the RAF:

"You've done well, Miss Watkins. I would never have expected you to make active service." He put me through his battery of tests. "There is something wrong, but it's not the heart, although it's putting a strain on the heart. For you, this is serious. You must go back to your station doctor and ask for another test."

By now I had been posted to RAF Langley, where we lived in the actors' orphanage. The very young woman doctor opened my file wearily, as though the weight of the world lay on her shoulders.

"You don't want sick leave, so what do you want?" At least she had read the previous doctor's notes.

"To find out what's wrong, and put it right! Dysentery is a very tiresome disease."

"I can assure you, you do not have dysentery and there's nothing wrong with you. At times in life one just has to pull oneself together and get on with it. Now I'm going to insist you take sick leave, two weeks of it!"

This time I was delighted. My grandmother had died and I was free to help Mother with all the dreary procedures. Then I accompanied her to Kent to arrange the family cottage. We were both so exhausted that on fine days we spent long afternoons lying in the bluebell woods, and we would talk to each other as we had done during the nights on the long sea voyage up the east coast of Africa, in the very early days of the war.

Events were happening in the world, the British election came and went, with the landslide to Labour. It was hard to believe that Churchill, who had brought us through the war, was not to be allowed to finish the job.

Three months earlier, while I was still at Caserta, two members of the Labour Party had come out electioneering. One had promised us a much speedier return home and faster demobilization if we voted Labour. One questioner asked if either side would be able to conjure up sufficient transport to return us all quickly. His question was dismissed as unimportant. My question was whether women would have full opportunities under a Labour Government. I was told this would be achieved by introducing a women's party, so that each constituency would fight a four-cornered election, with a Conservative, a Labour, a Liberal, and a Woman candidate. I was not impressed, but was clearly in the minority. The voters swept Labour to power.

Mother and I had been given tickets to the theatre – it was a show I wanted to see about servicewomen. There were three empty seats in front of us, very unusual in London at that time, when every theatre was crammed with men on leave. Churchill and his family came in after the lights had gone down, he did not want to be seen so soon after he had been defeated. Even so, he was recognized at once; the curtain, which had started to rise, was lowered and the entire theatre stood up and cheered. The cast came on stage in front of the curtain to join in the uproar. Then we all sang "For he's a jolly good fellow" at the tops of our voices. Tears ran down Winston's cheeks, his wife and daughter put their arms round him and led him to the three seats immediately in front of us. The curtain went up, the play went on.

In the interval, Mother leaned forward, introduced herself to Churchill and asked whom she should see in London about agricultural marketing of Kenya crops after the war. I was told to write down the names and addresses in the answer. I was in uniform and he smiled at me approvingly. I told him I had served with his daughter at TME.

The drama on the stage was nothing like as dramatic as our everyday life had been these last years. It consisted of an argument between a senior woman officer and the relatives she had harangued into looking after her child while she was away. Every time anyone suggested that she should not have gone to war, her place was in the home, and servicewomen had done nothing but get in the way, the whole theatre cheered. It was clear that the attitude to working women would be the same as the attitude to Churchill, a necessary evil in time of war, to be discarded as soon as peace came.

The papers were full of the terrible bombs dropped on Japan, and then came the relief of Japan's capitulation. It was so sudden, so unexpected, so terrible to see the pathetic skeletons of men emerging from the POW camps

"I don't believe it! I don't believe it" said my aunt. Throughout the war, with two sons and her husband on active service, she had never shown emotion, never wept at the frequent farewells. Now there were tears in her eyes. I had never seen her cry before. "The war is over and all three of my men are still there!"

The next time we went out together, we passed a telegraph boy, and for once she did not stop to see where he was going, but turned to me and said: "Is it not wonderful, to live without fear?"

No one commented then on the loss of life or the implications of the new and terrible weapon. The relief was all-pervading. At last the killing was over, the soldiers and the wretched survivors of the Japanese camps would soon be coming back. And there was relief that Hitler had not obtained the atomic bomb first – we all knew that he had been promising his people a secret weapon which would change the course of the war. There was more rejoicing, more parading through the streets, and more horror as the reality of what had happened became known.

Mother went back to Kenya and my aunt looked at me dubiously. She had made me some cotton frocks from curtain materials at the beginning of the summer – curtain material was the only stuff obtainable off the ration; the one I had on was in a weave as coarse as hessian. She was concerned that whereas it had fitted two months ago, it now hung empty and flapping.

"You must go and see someone who takes your illness seriously," she said. I insisted it was no good.

Then one evening, coming off duty fairly late, pushing my bicycle across the road, I fainted. Whoever picked me up took me straight to the MO's office and I was plonked on a couch while she was fetched. She was so sure that I was drunk, she did not even open my file. She rang the duty officer, who reported that I had left the office sober fifteen minutes earlier, and to his knowledge I had had no alcoholic drink that evening. By this time alcohol made me sick, presumably because the amoebae had reached my liver.

"Hoping for some more sick leave?" she asked. "Because I can assure you are not going to get it. I abhor lead-swingers."

I struggled to my feet and left. I had to cycle two miles to my digs; at least there was no black-out now. My aunt heard of this incident from one of my colleagues and was furious. She escorted me, protesting, back to Harley Street and insisted on coming into the consulting room with me. It was October, three months since my last visit. I told him what had happened when I fainted. He examined me with his usual care and wrote a note: "Take this, and give it to the young woman! I am quite sure you have some tropical bug and now you must not go back to work until you have been treated!"

I took the precaution of reading the letter myself before handing it over to her – it is always as well to know what to expect. He said that I was not lead-swinging, that my condition had deteriorated rapidly and if I fainted again I might not recover so easily. She would be responsible. She took a few seconds to gain control of herself:

"Who arranged for you to go to Group Captain Parsons-Smith?" The group captain was well known in the RAF.

"It's not the group captain, Ma'am, it's his father. He treated me before the war."

"Who said you could go to him?"

"I went of my own accord, because I had been his patient as a child."

"And who is paying?"

"I am!" No need to say he was treating me free.

"You know he wants you admitted to hospital?"

"Yes, Ma'am!"

"You know all beds are needed in the hospitals for sick people, really sick people, those coming back from Burma, for example." I did not say anything. "Well, I don't expect they'll have room for you." She picked up the phone. "No, certainly not a priority case," I heard her say. She turned to me triumphantly.

"It's November 6th before they can admit you! I hope not to see you before then." She picked up the letter to put it on my file, and noticed the bit about not going back to work. "Four weeks' sick leave, that suit you? That's what you wanted, isn't it?"

I fled. Sick leave is all very well if you have somewhere to go. I had not. I did not like sleeping in my aunt's sitting room all the time; even with the admiral away in Kiel she had other things to do than worry about me. I decided to go to Oxford, stay with Winifred who was doing a diploma in education, and do some reading. No chance now of taking the second exam for LMH, as I would be in hospital, but St. Anne's had an exam in the spring. It did not occur to me that LMH might have offered me a place on the first exam.

Taffy was still stationed in Italy. During the summer he had come on leave and had insisted on asking Mother down to meet his parents. Now he came on leave again and collected me. I was treated almost as a member of the family. Yet he had never proposed to me, never touched me, and only declared his love in the letters with which he continued to bombard me. He was full of all the things I should be doing to prepare for civvy street. He had very strong ideas about every detail of daily life, the clothes women should wear, the food one should eat, how a house should be furnished, how a kitchen should look, all of which he illustrated with sketches. I liked thinking about these things, and enjoyed answering his letters. Taffy in flesh and blood was different. He was critical, I was tetchy.

By now I was feeling extremely ill. Every minor activity – helping to get a meal, doing my own washing – had become an effort. Taffy had planned to take me on a week's trip around his favourite haunts, ending up in Cambridge – where he hoped to persuade me to go instead of Oxford. His mother now intervened; we were not to stay in the same hotels, it was bad for my reputation. The meaning behind the words came through clearly: if we slept together he would feel committed to me.

"We always stayed in the same place in Italy!" he said.

She turned to me: "How do you feel about this?"

I did not point out that we had never stayed at a hotel in Italy, merely in each other's messes, as was customary.

"Well, we could always stay in different hotels in the same place, if that would make us more respectable!" I suggested.

Taffy turned on me. "So that's how you feel?" he asked.

I wondered what I had said. "Taffy, I feel lousy and will be a poor companion. Take me to Cambridge on your next leave."

"That sounds a very sensible idea!" his mother said.

"As you are feeling so unwell I'll drop you off in London on my way to Cambridge!" He seemed to have forgotten that I wanted to go to Oxford, not London. I did not say anything.

When his mother said, "You will come and see us again, won't you?" I knew it was all over. Later, when I was in hospital, he sent me a letter saying he was too young to settle down. He never wrote again.

On the correct day I reported to the hospital, somewhat cowed by its size, by the sheer numbers of very sick and disabled men wandering about. The women's ward was the peacetime baby department. They started me on full tropical tests at once and two days later diagnosed amoebic dysentery, an enervating and unpleasant tropical infection which results in an ulcerated colon and, if left untreated as mine had been, to ulcers in other parts of the anatomy, including the liver. The standard treatment was injections of emetine, which imposes a strain on the heart. Parsons-Smith was consulted and forbade its use. So I had to have the alternative treatment. Every day for four weeks the foot of my bed was raised some inches above the head, and I was filled with a yatrin enema which I had to retain for ten hours. The yatrin was yellow and soon my skin, eyes and tongue were all yellow too. It stung as it was poured in, and throughout the treatment I had such cramps at night that I could not sleep. This was a recognized condition and sleeping pills had been prescribed.

The nursing was on the whole good, but there was one woman whom everyone dreaded. Her nickname was Sister Fearsome; she was the most unobservant woman I had ever met. She never noticed a change in anyone's condition, and would rarely accept there had been a change even when it was pointed out to her. We had all been conditioned by circumstance not to grumble about our own discomforts, but we would bring each others's to her attention: "X had a bad night, Y is in pain most of the time." My wardmates tried to bring home to her that I had bad nights and was in constant pain. She denied me the sleeping pills, saying they were unnecessary for a girl of my age. The lack of sleep and constant pain made me feel terrible. When the doctor realized what was going on, he put me on to morphine. It was wonderful to float away over all the troubles of the world.

On 21st December I was discharged from hospital. On reaching London I felt so weak that I decided to stay there for two nights before going down to my aunt, who had moved to her new house at Chichester. I stumbled into a women's hostel in Baker Street and collapsed into bed. The warden was wonderful, and insisted on sending special meals up to me. The following day I went to have my hair permed; the girl took one look at me and refused to touch my hair, saying I looked too ill. With some persuasion she washed and set it. My face looked awful and I hoped a facial might help. Elizabeth Arden had sent me cosmetics in Italy, but in Bond Street the girl refused to treat me. On a bus returning to Baker Street a woman old enough to be my mother insisted I take her seat. It was unnerving to have appearances so much against me, and not to be able to do anything about it.

My welcome down in Chichester was warm, but that first Christmas of the peace the house was cold and comfortless. It was still being decorated, and furniture was piled everywhere. One cousin was home by now, the other would soon follow. My uncle was on leave from Kiel, ill and on a special diet. We were still unaccustomed to life without domestic help and after ten minutes helping my aunt, I was exhausted. After Christmas I took myself off to Oxford.

In January I had to go back to hospital again. They decided to give me a D & C to try and cure the internal pains and cramps. A few days' rest in the warmth and comparative comfort of the hospital made me feel, and look, much better. One of the girls, Doris, who had been in hospital with me in November came back for a check-up. She had always been playing pranks on the Sisters and making us all laugh.

"You look so much better," she remarked, "that we're going to have some fun. When does Fearsome come on duty?"

"She's only gone for her tea-break before our supper is served." I said.

Doris led me into the bathroom, set my hair, and made up my face from her own box of cosmetics. Leaving me locked in the bathroom, she went round all the patients, officers and women, borrowing bits and pieces, a necklace here, earrings there, an elaborate hair comb, a smart satin house coat. She waited until Sister Fearsome came back from her tea-break, forced my feet into a pair of high-heeled shoes she had found abandoned in a cupboard, combed out my hair and led me tottering out.

"Hallo, Sister, here is Miss Kenya, the artiste I promised I would bring down. Are the girls ready for the concert?"

"Concert, what concert?"

"But I wrote about it, Sister, after our conversation in December. I said then I would arrange the concert, and here we are…"

"I didn't get any letter. I know nothing about it." Fearsome sounded wonderfully dismayed.

"Come on, Sister, we can't leave Miss Kenya standing here when she has come all this way. I'll take her in to the girls while you chase up the piano!" Sister still had not recognized me, nor did any of the girls in the twenty-bed ward, although I had visited them every day for the last week. We walked the full length of the ward, myself teetering in the ill-fitting shoes. Doris turned to me.

"Sing something you can sing without a piano – tell me what and I'll help out!"

"I told you, I can't sing – with or without a blasted piano!" Unabashed by my protests, Doris turned to face the girls.

"We are very fortunate to have the well-known singer and artiste with us tonight. Girls, give Miss Kenya a big hand!"

"I'll deal with you later!" I whispered and put on my sweetest smile for the girls. I pretended not to notice that my fellow inmates from the officers' ward had congregated in a giggling group by the entrance.

"It is a great pleasure to be with you tonight, girls. As I believe many of you come from Ireland, Scotland, Wales, and some of you from as far afield as Poland and Czechoslovakia, I am going to start with a demonstration of how the English sing." I launched straight into My Darling Clementine, one of the few songs whose words I could remember. My tuneless rendering of the tone deaf was drowned by the roars of laughter and applause. As soon as I had opened my mouth to speak, everyone had recognised me. As the laughter went on, Doris and I started laughing too. There was so much noise that we hardly noticed Sister come in with two porters trundling a piano. I put on my haughtiest expression, and stood looking down the room. The noise grew louder.

"Quiet, girls," screamed Sister, "how can Miss Kenya entertain you when you make such a noise! Quiet, I say!"

The noise redoubled as the girls realized that the joke was on Sister Fearsome. Even the porters had tumbled to the deception, for on my previous stay these two had often pushed me around in my bed. They too joined in, leaning one either end of the piano like bookends.

"What is the joke, tell me what is the joke?" Sister grasped the shoulders of the nearest patient and tried to shake her into submission as she repeated the question again and again in her high-pitched, irritable voice.

"Look at her! Don't you recognize her?" gasped the girl.

Sister looked, recognized, and understood. She was not amused. I looked round for the culprit, Doris. She had already crept out. Fortunately I too was leaving the next day.

The following week I had to sit six papers for the St. Anne's entrance exam in Oxford. I did not manage one of them without being sick in the middle. The invigilators were elderly men, retired dons. I think they felt so sorry for me that they put a mark on the papers that I was ill. That is the only way I have been able to explain the fact that St. Anne's offered me a place to read philosophy, politics and economics that October.

There was just seven months to fill in. I knew my demobilization number was getting much nearer. Passages to Kenya were too rare and too expensive to be considered, but I might be able to get to Austria. Otherwise I would have to take a job. It was nearly a year since I had done any work.

# Chapter 20
## Onward to Oxford

While I was in hospital, the RAF station at Langley had been closed down, the unit moved to RAF Medmenham near Henley. The WAAF mess was hutments in a bluebell wood, extremely chilly in that cold Spring, but wonderfully countrified. The Headquarters were in Medmenham Manor.

The cypher office had been set up in the butlers pantry so that we could use the silver safe. Not once did I take the cypher machines or books out of that safe, except to count them. There were no cyphers to do, the government ones were done in a special unit in Whitehall. We were paid, fed, and given all kinds of benefits, when our work in the services was no longer needed and employers were coming round to recruit us into civvy street.

There were so many interesting jobs on offer, far more than there had been before the war, or would be in three years time. Before my place at Oxford had been confirmed, I had interviews with the organization for the administration of occupied countries, two different charities working for refugees, and the civil service cyphers department who were recruiting candidates for India, to work on cabinet cyphers during the transition to independence. Three years later, the choice for women had narrowed to little more than had been on offer before the war.

One day my aunt rang up. She needed help urgently. Her nephew, five years younger than myself, had just joined the navy and was sailing to the Far East when he was taken ill with meningitis and died while at Singapore. She wanted to go to the other end of the country to comfort her sister, but my uncle had just been invalided home, needed care, and was on a difficult diet. As there was nothing to do, I was given a week's compassionate leave immediately.

It was hard work. I had never run a house before, and never had to turn minimal rations into an attractive diet. The jobbing gardener helped by producing delicious vegetables. When he came in with a basket of asparagus I did not have a clue what to do with it. I turned to the pre-1914 version of Mrs Beeton, the one which did not have a proper index because we poor fool women users would not how to use one. I opened the book at the vegetable section. It started: "*Always remember that it is the kitchen maid who deals with the vegetables, while the cook concentrates on the meat dish!*" Fortunately the arrival back home of one of the Admiral's son's after five years of war caused such happiness that I was no longer needed.

Back at my no-work, I put myself down for a one week's 'Brides Course', intended for those leaving to set up house. All the married women had been given priority and had been demobilized by this time, so there were vacancies on the course. It was held at Margate in a sea-side villa which the nine pupils had to run under instruction. As the only officer, I found myself on all the dirty jobs, floor-scrubbing and saucepan-scouring. We were given imaginary families of two young children, and a husband working a nine-hour day on the national average wage of £5 a week, and had to budget food, clothing, and housework round these facts. It was a good course, stressing that budgeting time is as important as budgeting money. The immediate benefits were that I could now cook a meal, clean a house, and had made myself a fetching dress in a deep pink angora wool.

We were given one day off to amuse ourselves, with transport to take us where we chose to go. The villa overlooked the sea and I had noticed that every time a small steamer passed the girls had all cried; "Oh, look at that big ship!" Most of the coastline had been out of bounds to civilians during the war; few of these young girls had ever visited the seaside, let alone seen any ocean going ships. I wanted them to see what big ships were like, to visit our wonderful navy.

"Let's go visit the navy at Chatham!" I said. Everyone was enthusiastic, even the kitchen staff and domestic science instructor decided to come along. Fortunately she had been a drill sergeant in an earlier life, and promised to march us all in. The driver who came to fetch us was wearing her best blues instead of the usual battle dress. She saluted me smartly:

"Ma'am, do you think I could come too, into the dock yard, I mean?"

"Yes, of course. Much depends on you. You have to get us conveniently near the main gate but parked so that we are not seen getting out of the truck. No visitors permits are being issued, so we shall use shock tactics. I'll sit in front with you, and we'll see what we can find."

We found a parking place out of sight of the main entry, and I gathered everyone round.

"Look, girls, we are going to march in as if we owned the place. I don't think anyone will stop us! Best foot forward and NO GIGGLING!"

The domestic science instructor lined us all up and off we marched. When we reached the corner near the guard house, we wheeled round to the left, the barrier shot up and we marched through, saluted by the guard. I was in front with the instructor and as I returned the salute, I noticed all eyes were on our legs. Silk stockings were as hard to come by as women in a dock yard, but every one of us was wearing them.

We marched straight along the nearest quays, past a destroyer, a couple of tugs, a mine sweeper, another destroyer, shrill wolf whistles following us as we passed.

"Where are we off to?" My colleague was an experienced marcher, and could carry on a conversation out of the side of her mouth.

"To the cruiser at the far end of the dock, unless I can see anything larger, when we shall divert course!"

"Why do you have to choose the furthest vessel?" she demanded.

"Because the bigger the ship, the better the tea! I'm not an admiral's niece for nothing."

"How do you know we'll be invited on board?"

"There are twelve young girls behind us, and several hundred bored seaman in that cruiser! What do you think?"

It was a warm day in late spring, our woollen uniforms were tight and hot, I could hear from the thudding feet behind us that the girls were getting tired of this long hot trek. When we arrived, our instructress halted and right-turned us. Before we could draw breath a smart rating ran down the gangway and saluted us.

"Officer-of-the-watch's compliments, miss, and what do you want?" He was eyeing us girls as hungrily as we were eyeing the ship. I was in no doubt about our tea.

"We would like to look round your boat, please. It's quite the smartest in the dock." I deliberately used the wrong word, 'boat' instead of 'ship'.

In five minutes we were on board, the girls shedding their hot jackets and caps on to a sea chest. They looked so much prettier, more feminine, in their blue shirts.

We had a splendid afternoon, everyone vying to show us his part of the ship. In groups of four we crawled down steel ladders into the engine room, looked at the neatly stacked hammocks and the places where they were hung at night, inspected the spotless galleys where they were already at work on our tea, gave suitable squeals of dismay when we were mock-locked in the cold storage rooms, sat in the gun pits and were shown how to swing the guns round, had an excellent sit-down meal – our number divided between the gun room and the petty officers' messes, then reassembled to climb more companion ways to the bridge.

The captain emerged to bid us goodbye. I recognised him at once but did not show it. He took me on one side.

"Tell me, did we send you an invitation to come?"

"I'm afraid not, sir," I admitted, "we had a day off and most of the girls had never seen a big ship before, and certainly never been on one. I thought they should learn about the Navy, so I just marched them in!"

"And nobody stopped you?"

"No, they saluted us! Kind and friendly all the way!"

He looked at me closely. "I've seen you before, in Egypt, was it?"

"Yes, sir, and the Seychelles."

"You girls get around. You were with Ferguson's outfit?"

I did not remind him that we had also met much more recently, at Christmas, at my uncle's house. The country south of Chichester was heavily colonized by senior naval officers. I was not sure that my uncle would approve my tactics, of getting a dozen WAAFs uninvited onto one of HM's ships.

There were still some weeks before my number came up. My final job was my first as an administrative officer. I was posted to an airfield near Thame which was closing down. It was on a peace time farm and I had a flat over the stables where I lived alone in state with an airwoman to wait on me. The officers' mess was in the main house, other ranks were housed in long rows of temporary hutments.

Every day the station became more desolate and the job less demanding, as we took the place to pieces bit by bit, listing and returning stores, repairing vehicles to be driven away, closing down and writing off all the temporary buildings. The hangars had been damaged in the winter storms and not repaired, the guard house had broken windows and a door hanging on one hinge, the sentry box had blown over.

It was not only the physical things that had changed. Most evenings I spent in the men's mess, and had plenty of time to notice that mess life, and the male officers, had changed even more. The old 'pops', with their chests full of War I medals and their interminable reminiscences, had all gone, the first to be demobilized. The wild young flying officers who had swung round on electric fan blades and peed into WAAF caps had suddenly become sober citizens. The future had always been a forbidden topic in the RAF, for not everyone would have one. Now for the first time in their adult lives they did have a future and they devoted much time to it. When do you get out? Are you going to university? Where are you going to live? How do you get a mortgage?

There was also serious courting to catch up on, not just fooling around with the nearest popsie but finding a suitable life companion. To assist in this task they spent their spare time scouring the countryside for off-the-ration food – a chicken from one farm, half a pint of cream from another, strawberries from a third. In those days you did not arrive on the girl's doorstep with flowers in your hand; you cannot eat flowers.

It was always a poignant moment when another demobilization took place, and the whole mess turned out to see him off. "Good luck! Happy Landings! Keep in touch!" Another friend dropped cheerfully from our lives.

Some left less happily. It was at Thame that for the first time I had to arrange for the discharge of pregnant airwomen. In those days it was a dreadful disgrace and there was a whole procedure set out as to how we should treat them, to prevent the episode from spoiling a girl's life. If she were under twenty-one (and by this time they nearly all were under twenty-one), her parents had to be told. If they refused to have her home – and most parents did because of the shame attached to having a baby without acquiring a husband first – sheltered accommodation had to be found. It was a tricky operation, demanding tact, sympathy and firmness. I was wonderfully helped by a motherly old sergeant who would stand behind each girl as I interviewed her, drying her tears when necessary, and explaining to me the particular circumstances of each case.

When the sergeant was in turn demobbed and replaced by an Oxford graduate only a little older than myself, I felt quite lost. It was then that a girl came before me who should not have come at all. She had been kissed on the cheek by a soldier who had befriended her on a railway platform and was convinced she would have a baby, for her mother had told her that kisses were dangerous and led to babies. She produced all the symptoms. I lent her my copy of Marie Stopes, one of the few books one could buy on the subject in those days. She never returned it.

At last my turn came to climb into the truck which would take me to Oxford Station and so to RAF Wythall, near Birmingham, for my demobilization. I had looked forward to this moment with acute anticipation; yet the next day, when I walked out of the huge demob hall with a fistful of civilian papers in one hand and a railway voucher in the other, I was overwhelmed by a sense of loss. I no longer had the right to wear uniform, a uniform which for four long years had signified that I belonged to a widespread, supportive and much respected family, the air force.

My uncle had now retired, and had gone to Austria for the summer to reclaim my grandmother's house. I hoped to join him, but I must first make arrangements for next term. In the train back to Oxford I had bought a newspaper and glanced at the date. It was my twenty-third birthday. Birthdays had been good moments. For my nineteenth there had been warm champagne atop the Great Pyramid; for my twentieth the cutting of the WAAF's own birthday cake on one of the hottest nights of a hot Egyptian summer; for my twenty-first an operational flight from Mombasa to the Seychelles, and last year Shakespeare in Stratford.

Yet the strange dream world of wartime life had roller-coastered me into nightmare more often than I cared to remember. There were the casualty lists from our squadrons streaming out of my cypher machine as the sweat poured out of my body in that sweltering summer of the

Great Flap in Cairo; the long walk back from my father's grave, my heel pulsing with pain; the view from the balcony in the Seychelles as the Catalina roared past me and turned turtle; the listening and calling, calling and listening from that same balcony to the deathly quiet airways for the crooning Canadian voice: 'You're the new one, honey, I'm coming in to see you right now!'; the Italian airfield with the skidding aircraft exploding in front of me, permeating the air with the sweet smell of burning human flesh; the reconnaissance pictures of the Austrian village of my youth flickering on the screen; showing it bombed to smithereens; the ship's cabin where six women lay wedged in bunks through endless hours listening to the depth charges around us, wondering who had copped it.

As I left the train at Oxford station I thought I was moving from that dream world to real life. It was only later that I learned about ivory towers. I went straight to the telephone and waited my turn. In my ignorance I had not realized that term ended so soon. Winifred had gone down and her digs had closed. The old hostel where I had stayed had gone back to being the Carlton Club. Tonight, the first night of my demobilization, I had nowhere to go.

Retrieving my bicycle, I turned up Hythe Bridge Street, crossed the canal and turned into Beaumont Street then St Giles. Oxford had been untouched by bombs on the express orders of Hitler, who wanted the place with all its collegiate buildings for his regional government of Britain. It looked more lovely than ever on the afternoon of a lovely June day, every tree in full fig, every suburban garden ablaze with colour, every wall intact. There was very little traffic, and cycling along the empty roads made my heart sing.

I had already marked the addresses of landladies recommended by my college on a map and now intended to work through them. They were all in North Oxford so I would cycle out by the Banbury Road and return by the Woodstock Road. Somewhere along the way I would find a bed and breakfast place to sleep. The first landlady looked me up and down and explained that she was sorry, but she didn't fancy any ex-service girls, nothing personal mind, but they know too much, if you know what I mean. She gave me a coy wink and closed the door. The second explained that she liked people to write first and call afterwards. The third wanted to know why my father was not making arrangements for me and wanted him to guarantee my bill, while it was my mother who interested the fourth, as she tut-tutted over the iniquity of a girl making her own arrangements. Obviously I must be a liar, widow women just did not farm coffee on their own in Kenya.

On my list was one address, 64 Woodstock Road, with the remark 'full' pencilled against it. On my return journey I was right outside the house and on a whim decided to call in. Before I had even reached the door, it opened and a yappy Cairn terrier waddled out and nipped my ankle. I picked up the fat little creature and put it under my arm, the nippy end where it could do no harm. It seemed quite happy while I spoke to the elderly lady who followed. She was very thin, there was no doubt who was getting the rations in her house. When I told her what I wanted she said: "What a coincidence. I have just received this letter by the afternoon post, cancelling a booking!" *No wonder*, I thought as she took it from me, *with that dog around*. But then she added that she liked to have older girls as they were usually more responsible, and yes, there was plenty of room to leave my luggage and bicycle until term started, and why did I not join her for a cup of tea while I considered the small ground floor room she had just shown me. It was a small room and looked out onto a brick wall, but my mind was made up. It was not a decision I ever regretted.

It had been a lonely way of spending a birthday. I had not seen one person I knew. There was too much time to think and I wondered if civvy street was ready for us, we who had become adults in the war, independent, unread, ignorant and uncouth as we were. Five long years and nothing learned, nothing of much use in civvy street. Yet collectively we had achieved so much. On that lovely June day, Oxford was a beautiful university town waiting to cast its spell once again over a generation of veterans. It was not, as Hitler had planned, the headquarters of the German Administration.

Now I had to take my first steps into the world of peace, unprotected by a uniform, and with no immediate family. With the return of their sons to their home, my uncle and aunt seemed to have lost interest in me, although my uncle had obtained for me a pass to visit Austria. Austria was under Allied occupation, divided into four zones with one of the four main Allies in charge of each. The Tyrol lay in the French zone, a singularly unhappy arrangement for the Tyroleans, who had hated the

French with a fierce, pent-up hatred since Napoleon had beaten them more than a century earlier. However, the French General kindly welcomed the British Admiral (my uncle) to reclaim his old home. I was to go along in the baggage, but it proved more complicated than I had thought. To travel in Europe was to revert to wartime conditions.

It took three days to get my papers in order and to book a ticket; and another three days to complete the journey in slow trains across Europe, on some stretches so jam packed that any movement was impossible for twelve hours at a time. At last we were chugging down the Inn valley, where our bombing had been all too thorough. Every station was now a pile of rubble beside a temporary hut, every bridge across the river a temporary one to be crossed at walking pace. The windows were board up, so I stood by the door and was the first to jump out at Brixlegg, excitement welling up in me at the glimpse of familiar scenery. I confronted guiltily the pile of rubble that had been a pretty little station. Before I had my luggage down from the train the porter was beside me, hugging me and saying, "Die Olga! Die Olga!" again and again. It was my mother's name.

"I brought her luggage down from the castle, the day she left to go to Africa!" he said. "It was in…"

"Nineteen-fourteen, ten years before I was born !" I interspersed

"How is she? When is she coming? I'll bring your luggage up for you this afternoon. I cannot come now, the junior porter did… did not come back…" His voice tailed off.

"This afternoon will be fine," I said, and meant it. I wanted to savour this minute alone, the adult returning to her childhood paradise. I wanted time to recall my father taking me for long walks, my grandmother welcoming us home again. Neither was alive now.

# Chapter 21
## Austrian Interlude

At the beginning of the village the shoemaker's shop no longer stood, but there was a party of twenty assorted young people of all colours and races digging out the cellar. Curious, I paused to watch. They were talking English. I asked a tall white man wearing the long orange robe of a Buddhist monk what they were doing. They belonged to a voluntary organization financed by the Quakers to rebuild Europe, and they were rebuilding the cobbler's shop. It had been hit because it was so near the station. Other damage had been done in the village, the church wore the onion on top of its spire at a rakish angle, walls had come down here, roofs had been damaged somewhere else. Gaps in the neat rows of houses had been replaced with wooden sheds from which the business was run. A number of people recognized me and came out for a chat, and the reply to "Wie Gehts?" was always the same: "Es geht schön, es müss gehen!" (literally: "It goes all right, it must go!" or in other words: "Things are pretty bad but I have to cope and I can do so.")

On through the park and up through the trees to where the old castle stood, west-facing with snow-covered mountains in the distance. It was all so much more beautiful than I remembered. My fingers found the secret catch on the wrought-iron gate and let me in. I went upstairs to my family's rooms. Everything was in wonderful order, floor and furniture gleamed, the bath – comfortably settled in the kitchen –shone, my bed had been made up. I stood in the window, lost in the wonder of it all, and then realized I suffered from the same complaint as my grandfather – I hated to look at mountains I had not climbed.

I spotted a lone car creeping along the road from Innsbruck. It was my uncle coming back. That evening it was made clear to me that I would be welcome to join them at meals, but not on family expeditions, there would be no room in the car. I must amuse myself. I could hardly believe my luck. I had three whole months to climb all those mountains I had been looking at, with no social responsibilities at all.

I would pack Mother's old rucksack with a change of blouse and socks, shove into it as many tins of food as I could carry, put on her walking boots, take up the alpine stock I had been given as a child, and disappear for days at a time. After years of living in close quarters with numbers of others, sharing bedrooms, working in crowded offices, I needed to be alone, to have time to myself. I struggled up steep mountain paths and trudged contentedly along ridges, surprised to find a welcome wherever I went.

It is a proud thing to be a bauer, a yeoman farmer, in the Tyrol. Every summer the cattle are sent up to the high pastures, the alms, to preserve the grass lower down to make hay for the winter. Traditionally the old men and the young girls take the cattle up, while the rest of the family tackle the heavier work of cultivation in the valleys. The alm huts had always been places for walkers to rest, to obtain milk and cheese, to spend the night in the hay stored above the cow byre. Even so, I was hesitant to do this, thinking their need for the food was greater than mine, that English visitors would not be welcome so soon after the war. I soon learned differently.

On one perfect day in July, I was passing a high alm hut. An old man sat on the bench outside, drowning the sweet smell of hay with foul-smelling tobacco in a long pipe with a china bowl, enjoying the wonderful panorama all round him, and listening to the cacophony of cow bells which told his accustomed ear exactly where each cow was, what she was up to.

"Where art thou going, young woman?" he called out to me.

"Walking; I'm on holiday!"

"Dost thou not want a drink of milk?"

"Yes please." I was happy to notice a wooden stand placed to unload heavy rucksacks; I off-loaded mine and, still holding my alpine stock, went over to his bench. He looked at me carefully.

"Thou art not one of us!" His expression told me that my dress was acceptable but not my German.

"No. I'm English, a student."

"The English are always welcome," he said, "but not the cursed French!" The French were not generous victors.

The old man was staring down the valley. Far beneath us, we could see where the Ziller River flowed into the River Inn. He took up my alpine stock and pointed it at the Ziller Bridge.

"That," he said with pride, "is where we defeated Napoleon's army! Under Andreas Hofer!"

So famous were the exploits of Andreas Hofer in the Napoleonic wars of long ago that he became a symbol of Tyrolean unity and a statue had been erected to him in Innsbruck. When South Tyrol was awarded to Italy in 1918, the statue had been put into mourning. In 1946 it had already been wearing black for thirty years. It was doubly galling for Tyrol to be under French military occupation, and to have no hope of reuniting with South Tyrol.

The old man's hand passed over the silver band on my stick and he held it at a distance from long-sighted eyes to try and read the inscription. His arm was only just long enough to enable him to distinguish the two words on it, my name spelt the German way: "Elisabet" and "Matzen". It was a gift from my grandmother and she always called me by my first name. June, she would say, was not a proper name.

"And when does the Gnädige Fraulein start at Oxford?" I looked at him in astonishment. Had I mentioned Oxford? And why had he changed his mode of address from 'Mädchen' and the familiar 'thou' to 'Gnädige Fraulein' and the respectful third person used only to priests and aristocrats?

"How do you know I go to Oxford?" I asked. "We have many universities in England."

"Quite so, but our Gnädige Frau's granddaughters would only go to the best! Your old lady was one of the good women of this world. I wish you well. Take care! There is danger about."

"Are the mountains so dangerous then?"

"Not the mountains, it is the men who are dangerous!"

"The men? Who offer passing strangers milk?" I smiled questioningly.

"No," he said, "the men who are escaping, from there" – he pointed my stick north towards Germany – "to there!" My stick swivelled round until it pointed due south. "Up the Zillertal and so into Italy. On their way to South America!" He spat hard, neatly, so the tobacco-stained gob arrived between his feet and mine. He wanted me to know what he felt about the Germans. "If they found you were English, they would murder you! And no one would ever know!"

"Is that why I feel I am being followed, hear whistling from above me and then from below?"

"Yes. Your disguise is good, but try to avoid the main routes south! Walk east to west instead, you will be safer."

Then the conversation took a more practical turn.

"Do you need potatoes this winter? If you give me your watch I will guarantee you enough potatoes to feed four people through the winter!"

"But what do you want with this watch?" It was a large one, a man's airforce model, sturdy and practical but of no great value.

"Look here!" He led me into the smoky alm hut and felt along the beam above his wooden bed. Out came a coloured handkerchief and in it lay a dozen good watches, all makes and designs.

"This one," he said, picking out a dainty French model in gold, "is for my eldest granddaughter, and this" – his hand was on a German air force issue – "is for my grandson." He allocated each to its future owner.

"And mine?"

"Yours is for my son-in-law! He has just come back from a British prison camp and we get tired of hearing how good things were!" He laughed. I thought of the caretaker at Matzen with her two young children and poorly husband and of the long cold winter ahead of them. And some Austrian cousins would be there too, a family of three. They would all need potatoes far more than I needed a watch "Make it seven people and the watch is yours!"

His eyes went over me, looking for something else for which to bargain. "The watch and the rucksack?" he suggested.

"No, not the rucksack. It is my mother's, and was her mother's before that. Let us say potatoes for six people!" I held out my hand to signify I would make no more demands.

"The Gnädige Fraulein drives a hard bargain!" he said, grinning as he wrapped a huge hand round mine and squeezed until I nearly cried out. I hope the son-in-law enjoyed the watch. Sixty years later, those potatoes are still remembered.

When the old man asked me to stay the night, I agreed with alacrity, and sat with him and two of his granddaughters, all of us toasting our feet in the hole in the middle of the hut which contained a smoky wood fire. Over it the girls used a huge black frying pan to make schmarn, a rich and filling pancake far tastier than my contribution, a large tin of English sausages which we toasted over the fire and ate with our fingers.

Early next morning I took the old man's advice and set my course due East, and walked straight into another adventure. My path descended rapidly into the Ziller Valley, I hitched a lift which took me across the valley and the river, and then walked upstream until I found a twisting cart track to climb a valley up the east wall of mountains. When the cart road ran out I followed a mountain stream through pine woods. Marchental, Fairy Valley, my map called it. It was such a fairyland of peace and beauty that I almost regretted my decision to go to Oxford, for to do so I had turned down the offer of a job with an aid agency in Austria. The mountains, the scenery, the streams bubbling through pine forests, the intoxicating air, the friendliness of the people all went to my head. I wanted more time to enjoy it.

The path took me up to the top of the pass, the watershed for three valleys. I turned north into the Alpbach Valley, which would take me home, but the distance was further than it looked. At Inner Alpbach I halted for the night, sleeping for once in a bed rather than in a hay loft.

"You must come up next month," said the innkeeper. "There is a students' conference, international students from all over the world."

This was intriguing. I came up to have a look, and stayed for two weeks. Alpbach was then a tiny village tucked into a distant valley, famous for its picturesque housing and old world atmosphere. Yet here were students from all over Europe earnestly and endlessly discussing the future of the world. People who had recently been killing one another were now talking and playing together.

The variety of students was infinite. There were the two sons of the German philosopher Keyserling, the man who at the time of the Russian Revolution had propounded that a European elitist class should combine to counter the revolutionary spirit. They were young, handsome and arrogant as they recited Keyserling ideas. There was a very young and beautiful Italian princess dressed in a flour sack tied at her narrow waist with a piece of string, chestnut hair cascading down her back, rough sandals on her pretty bare feet. Most of us were endeavouring to maintain pre-war standards on post-war clothing shortages; only she had the brains, bravado and beauty to make the most of shortages. She looked stunning.

A great clumsy Russian fellow invited eight of us to his room to play the game "I drink to the health of Cardinal Hoth", which involved pouring glass after glass of neat vodka down one's throat. He had of course the strongest head of us all, but not strong enough to discover how I managed to remain sober – a simple matter of sitting in a corner of the room near the wash basin, so the vodka could be poured away and I 'drank' from an empty glass.

The most intriguing thing was the number of proposals of marriage I received. I could not understand why. Certainly on this wonderful holiday my health was rapidly returning, the dirndl dresses suited me admirably, but even so, twenty proposals – not propositions but proper proposals, made without any encouragement on my part – were inexplicable. That is, until I met Betty. Betty was an American girl whose small neat features were overwhelmed by a helmet of dark hair so thick it seemed to weigh down on her. She was also the only person at that conference who was overweight, and would ask lucky friends back to her room for feasts of imported delicacies.

We happened to be sitting at the same table one evening, and when a dancing partner brought me back, she heard me say, "Thank you. Ask me again in three years' time when I've finished my degree – and see if we're both still interested." As soon as the young man had gone Betty said:

"Was that a proposal of marriage? How many?" And when I told her, she told me she had had twice as many. "I guess you're Miss British Passport 1946 just as I'm Miss American Passport!"

"What do you mean?"

"Honey, it's not you they want to marry. It's the passport of your country they want, to escape the mess and squalor of Europe. If they can marry a pretty girl into the bargain, and use her family as the kicking-off point to a better life, so much the better!"

One young man, Toni, had not proposed but had shown his liking for me by planning outings to my taste. He was the same age as I, part

Jewish, and as a boy had been sent to prison for refusing to join a Nazi youth group. From there, at the age of seventeen, he had been recruited for fighting on the Russian Front. He had escaped, engineered his own 'death', taken a new name, and worked for the Resistance, frequently crossing into Italy and Switzerland by little-known mountain passes, to contact the Allies. I remembered that I had seen signals about him, and surprised him by using his code name. Now, in that same scenario of deep valleys and high mountains, we walked and talked of all the things we had done and seen.

On the night of the equinox full moon we had danced until midnight and then, with a party of others, we climbed the highest peak in the neighbourhood, reaching the top just as the sun turned the distant peaks first pink, then gold. We sat on the rocks shivering, too tired to go on walking, too cold to enjoy sitting still. The valleys below us were filled with clouds corrugated like wave marks on the shore. Cow bells echoed around us as the cows gathered in the alms to be milked. It was as if we were floating on a magic carpet above the troubles of the world. I wanted to stay there, walking in the Tyrolean Alps, for the rest of my life.

After that, we did several long walks together, Toni and I, sleeping in alm huts, washing in streams, buying food from the farmers. After a walk which lasted a week, we ended up back at Matzen. My uncle did not approve.

"How can you run about with an Austrian boy so soon after the war? Haven't you read about the camps, the terrible things that happened?" He was growing deafer than ever and always shouted now.

"This man is one of the bravest I've ever met. He fought for us, for the Resistance. His family suffered terribly because of him!" I shouted back

"You mean, you – an ex-officer of his Majesty's Forces – are running around with a traitor!"

Before leaving Austria, I went to say goodbye to my mother's cousin who had occupied our rooms in Matzen after he had been bombed out in Vienna. He had been a colonel in the Austrian Army after the First World War and, like many military men, had welcomed Hitler's invasion of Austria as the only possible solution to her economic problems. Matzen stood directly on the main supply route from Germany to Italy.

"How did the peace come" I asked him. He spoke English with a soft Irish brogue – his grandmother, my great grandmother, had been Irish, and he told me the story.

"Every morning I went up the tower with my binoculars to see what I could see, and every morning it was the same. The roads were crowded, traffic flowing steadily morning, noon and night in both directions. Train after train were running in both directions. No private vehicles on the road, no ordinary citizens on the trains.

"Then one morning traffic going south to the Brenner stopped, and all the traffic was coming one way, returning to Germany. I knew this meant the end. For three days the roads were crammed with a motorcade of soldiers, tired, shabby, defeated men, crawling back home down the valley. One morning there was a break, and then another procession started – I saw an American flag. I went downstairs and fetched your grandmother's Union Jack, the one she used to fly, and I climbed back up to hang it over the balcony on the top of the tower. Then I realized the traffic had stopped. I looked again, the vehicles had stopped moving, and most of the ones I could see were American!

"I hurried downstairs with the flag over my arm, right down through the lowest courtyard and onto the main road. There was a German colonel standing facing an American colonel in the main road, by the pub gate. Holding the flag in front of me, I went forward and said to the American: 'Excuse me, sir, but can I interpret for you?'

"He said, 'Yes, you are just the man I need. Tell him I accept his white flag, his surrender. Then tell him he has to clear the road of all the stationary vehicles. He can push them off the road onto the grass, anywhere he likes, but I want that road cleared immediately.' The two men shook hands and as they did so a young German boy in uniform raised his gun and aimed at the general. An American killed him immediately, before he could fire. The American colonel turned to me. 'Tell him to pile all those weapons up here – immediately. Armed men will be shot!' Then he asked: 'Can we take over the castle – it looks as if it would have enough accommodation for my unit.'

"I pointed out the disadvantages, the interior was all courtyards, empty space. It was an ancient monument under protection – the German military have not been allowed to use it. It belonged to an English naval officer. And it had a poor water supply. But then I told them about the park down below, they could camp there. There is fresh water from two springs , shelter for tents under the trees, room for vehicles as well as men. As soon as they started settling in, I sent my two grandsons, to whom I had been teaching English, down to offer their help, run messages, interpret, show them about the place. And they came back with armfuls of food. We were so hungry, we were gathering snails in the garden. Your grandfather always said the Americans were so generous, and I found it to be true. It was hard to see the boys so hungry."

So the war was over at last, and I must go back and learn to live in peace. How lucky I had been in my life so far. I felt humbled by the suffering of others. And even today, every morning as I greet a new day, I think of those who did not come back, whose lives closed before they had lived.

# A survivor says thank you

Trapped in the hours of my early fate,
I get up early and go to bed late,
Sleep is not welcome: I can explain,
It still brings dreams of a pranging plane.


Filled with the glory of  new born day,
I must get up early a prayer to say:
"Thank you, Lord, for the courage you gave,
"We all risked our futures our freedom to save.


"Thank you for the years we were spared,
"The work we have done, the children we reared,
"The people we've met , the places we've been,
"The friends we've made, the wonders we've seen.


"We, The survivors, must thank most the few,
"Who never came back their lives to renew,
"Bless their souls, and remember today
"We owe them a debt we can never repay!"

Elizabeth Watkins

# Lament after night ÐUty

*This was written in Cairo at the time of Alamein by
an eighteen year old WAAF*

She tossed in a room which was stifling hot,
She wanted to sleep but her muse said not.
"I came of this morning, I go on tonight,
"A dog is barking with all his might,
"I wonder why the shouting began,
"Between the bearer and laundry-man."


A ropey muse whose powers of verse,
Daily grow distinctly worse,
Even his prose is becoming cat.three,
He spoke to the WAAF, "Look WAAF" said he,
"Forget the flies and the yapping terrier,
"Forget the heat and bellicose bearer.


"Think yourself where you'd like to be
"If the war were past and you were free.
"Would you go on a long pleasure cruise?
"Would you write a book to air your views?
"Would you go travelling far from home,
Peking and Paris, New York and Rome?"

"Muse, " said the WAAF, "If you are asking me,
"I don't give a damn where e'er I be,
"I really don't care about what I may do,
"I don't even mind what happens to you.
"When God created the earth and the deep,
"He also created the night for sleep.


"For three long years I have sat up at night,
"And looked for the dawn and longed for the light.
"The only thing of which I am sure
"In the balmy days which follow the war,
"I'll go to bed early and get up late
"And be but a straw in the hands of fate.
"She can toss me uncaring from shore to sea,
"In the arms of Orpheus contented I'll be!"


*Sixty years in-the-fast lane later, I have discovered life is not like that. There were years of babies needing attention at night, a husband needing transport to and from airports, work needing the midnight oil, dogs whining to go out, cats yowling to come in, and on one occasion during Mau Mau two drunken guards fighting over the privilege of guarding me while my husband was away. Sleep was always sparse. So when I came across this poem again, I wrote a short sequel...*